Connecting Us

Connecting Us

Develop the engaged, goal-kicking team you've always dreamed of.

By
Maree Burgess

First published in 2018 by Maree Burgess in Melbourne, Australia.
© Maree Burgess
www.mareeburgess.com
All rights reserved. Except as permitted under the Australian Copyright Act 1968 (for example, a fair dealing for the purposes of study, research, criticism or review), no part of this book may be reproduced, stored in a retrieval system, communicated or transmitted in any form or by any means without prior written permission of the copyright owner, except as provided by international copyright law.

Illustrations by Maree Burgess
Conversational Dashboard™ image Judith E. Glaser
Cover illustration by Matt Emery
Edited by Nicola Dunnicliff-Wells, A Story to Tell

National Library of Australia Cataloguing-in-Publication data:

Author:	Maree Burgess
	Title: Connecting Us: Develop the engaged, goal-kicking team you've always dreamed of
ISBN:	978-0-6488165-0-8
Subjects:	Engagement
	Leadership
	Teams and teamwork
	Conversations

Disclaimer. The information in this book is provided and sold with the knowledge that the author does not offer any legal or other professional advice. It is not intended to provide specific guidance for particular circumstances and it should not be relied on as the basis for any decision to take action or not take action on any matter that it covers. Readers should obtain professional advice where appropriate, before making any such decision. To the maximum extent permitted by law, the author disclaims all responsibility and liability to any person, arising directly or indirectly from any person taking or not taking action based on the information in this publication.

Contents

Foreword vii
Acknowledgments xi
About the Author xiii
Introduction xvii

PART 1 - ME   1

   1 AWARE 3
   2. ADAPT 25
   3. COMMIT 39

PART 2 - THEM   41

   4. ENGAGE 51
   5. FLEXIBILITY AND AGILITY 79

PART 3 - US   81

   6. TRUST 93
   7. CONNECT 105
   8. US-CENTRIC 125

NEXT STEPS 127
SOURCES 129

Foreword

Three friends – Maree, Maria and me.

Dinner at a fancy restaurant.

A glass of wine and giggles.

Then, like a chilling breeze, the tone of the conversation suddenly became more serious.

"The team I'm in is out to get me", Maria said mournfully.

The fact is – we've all felt like this at some stage in our lives. Either we work far too hard and carry the brunt of the effort, or some control-freak takes over, and brutally asserts their will. If we're the team leader, managing these dynamics is just as hard as getting a successful outcome for our team and the organisation.

You know it and I know it. It's enough to make you storm off in a huff next time you have to lead a group, isn't it!

But it doesn't have to be that way. There is a better way. A more effective way.

A way of harnessing the power of the team so that everyone benefits, goals are kicked, and every member feels fulfilled and gratified.

But, how can you hit this lofty goal?

As a leader, how can you balance the demands of work, and the needs of the team?

That's why you're here, isn't it!

Well, you may have read Maree Burgess's earlier book 'The XX Project'. You may have even been to one of her outstanding workshops or seminars. But her new book... THIS book... is like nothing you've ever seen before.

At risk of sounding too dramatic, if you get good at these skills... it might just save your life.

Did you know that 75% of airline crashes occur when the aircrew are working together for the first time? Shocking, isn't it.

That's the power of an effective team. And that's what Maree is offering you in her new, easy-to-read, easier-to-implement book.

She wants you to develop the engaged, goal-kicking team you've always dreamed of.

You deserve it.

Heck, you've been planning for this since the beginning of your career. So, now it's your chance to achieve this once and for all.

Maree's book will get you there.

And Maria... our bedraggled team mate from the dinner I mentioned... what happened to Maria? Maree gave her such sterling advice it literally changed the way Maria viewed her team. I was there. I witnessed it.

And that, in its seed form, was the basis of this new book from the skilled and talented Maree Burgess.

Louise Bedford
Director www.tradinggame.com.au.
Best-selling author of 5 books about the sharemarket Trading Secrets
- Let the Trade Wins Flow
- The Secret of Writing Options
- The Secret of Candlestick Charting
- Charting Secrets

Acknowledgments

I would like to thank my family – Tony, Callon and Rhys, who support me and inspire me every day to lift my game.

Nicola Dunnicliff-Wells from A Story, you challenged my thinking and created order out of chaos and this book is a reality because of you.

To Matt Emery, who designed my cover, even with very little input from me – thanks for being flexibly creative.

Donna McGeorge - you generously provided your scarce time to read what I thought was a final draft and made some key edit suggestions and pushed me to a publishing deadline.

To my dear friends Tracey Ezard, Donna McGeorge and Deb Dalziel for being my sounding board, cheer squad and always having my back.

My thanks to Judith E. Glaser, who introduced me to Conversational Intelligence and made me realise that I help teams change their culture to something better.

About the Author

Maree is passionate about helping others collaborate, work and play well together.

She has helped leaders, teams and organisations throughout Australia learn how to communicate more effectively to get the results they are looking for to build engagement, lift performance and move through change.

Maree has a broad CV encompassing multiple careers: starting with a stint in a rural Forestry Commission where she leased bee sites and tracked tree felling; becoming a registered nurse at a major Melbourne trauma hospital; holding a variety of roles in banking and finance; and in 2003 finally working out what she wanted to do when she grew up!

That was when she started her own business, helping leaders and teams make change happen and develop the type of cultures that people want to be part of.

The 'The XX Project - Giving women the skills and confidence to step up in corporate' was published in 2015 and focuses on building a pipeline of women who are ready to step up into more senior roles.

Maree's superpower is to help people craft their own individual why.

INTRODUCTION

Introduction

Do you ever feel like leading a team is hit or miss? Sometimes you have a great team who get on well and do a terrific job. But are there times when a couple of people in your team are a bit toxic?

We spend a large majority of our life at work, with people that we see more of than our family and friends. It is an absolute joy to be part of a focused and functional team where the whole is greater than the sum of its parts and high levels of trust between team members exists; it is completely disempowering to be part of a toxic team where infighting is rife, people leave and knowledge is lost.

I've changed my career several times during my working life. I have sometimes lucked into awesome teams, and other times, ended up in teams not so awesome. I became curious about why teams were so different, and what could help a team change for the better.

This led to my business: working with leaders and teams to help them become more awesome. I know that it's possible to create an exciting and invigorating work environment. I have guided others as they have built teams of people who are energised, who learn from each other, and who look forward to hanging out together every day.

While it's your role, as team leader, to drive change towards the culture you want to be part of, each person in the team can – and, ideally, should – be involved.

Building a team's culture is like building a bridge: without a strong foundation and sound engineering, it may fail.

It begins with understanding the building blocks: relationships.

This book will help you identify and create the type of culture you want to be part of. Focusing on relationships within teams, it covers tools and strategies to build strong and resilient teams that are capable of performing at the highest level.

You'll find out how to make meetings productive and harmonious, how to generate positive outcomes from difficult conversations, and how you can work productively even with someone you don't like.

Moving from manic to magic

To begin with, you need to identify where you are. Figure 1, the manic-to-magic model describes teams at six stages from toxic to dynamic. Where are you on this model? Where is the team? Where do you and your team aspire to be, and how can you get there?

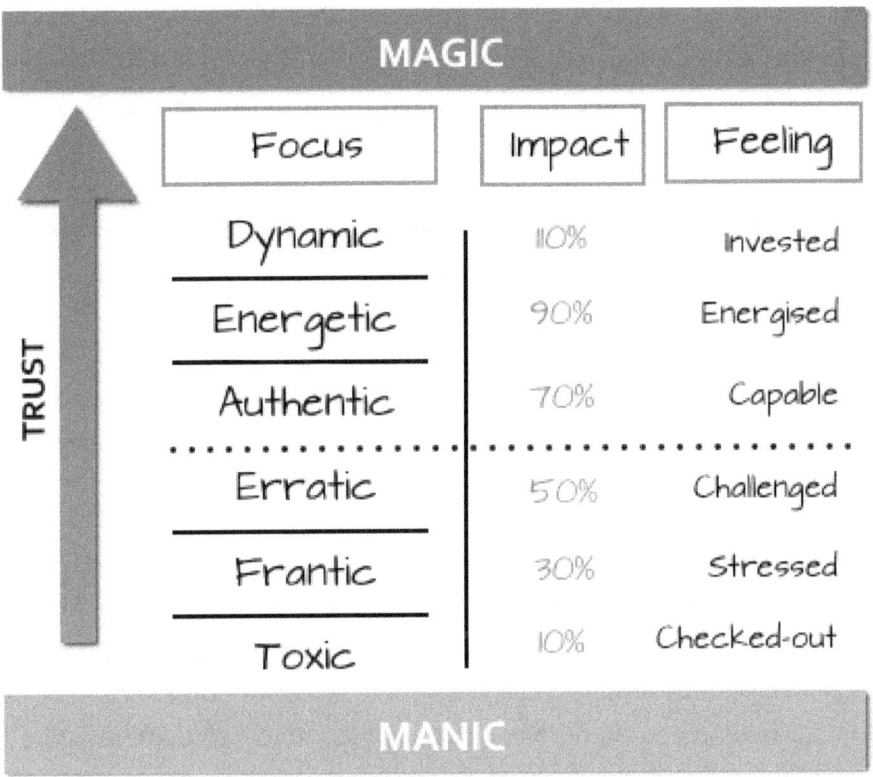

Figure 1: The Manic to Magic Model

At the bottom of the model, the **toxic team** sucks energy. Team members don't look forward to work; they live under a cloud of anxiousness that can become debilitating.

Strengths and values are not understood and certainly not considered. Lower performers (or under performers) are not supported; high performers become addicted to being right and create a clique of supporters around them. This group may even bully lower performers or those they dislike. The leader may exert their seniority over those who report to them.

Trust is low, and there may be infighting. Passive aggressive behaviour is rife and sabotage (of others within or outside the team) may exist. People leave – either they're unhappy, or they're asked to go – and knowledge is lost.

As a whole, the team is checked out and cannot see the bigger picture of how they fit within their organisation.

A toxic culture can be likened to a bad relationship: we know it isn't healthy but the thought of moving or changing seems too hard. We become to numb to how bad it actually is, so we tolerate unacceptable behaviour.

The *frantic team* is too busy being busy. It either has too much to do, or spends too much time fixing problems; there is no opportunity to think about working on the business. The team leader or organisation may have unrealistic expectations about what the team is capable of. The resulting stress further limits people's ability to think effectively and get stuff done.

A frantic team doesn't have time to build internal relationships, so hidden agendas and second-guessing are common. Trust is low, and people focus on surviving.

The *erratic team* sometimes performs well; other times, not so well.

This team may feel productive, but is often simply busy for the sake of being busy: it may have lost sight of what is important.

Being erratic can mean that relationship building does not happen with this team, as there isn't time. Yet, trust exists to some extent. Some workload sharing occurs and, mostly, everyone contributes. They focus on performance, but results are inconsistent.

The **_authentic team_** is on track, efficient, and gets the work done well without fuss. It does what is expected, though little more. Rather than think creatively, this team gets on with the job of delivering products and services to a good standard, as expected.

Leadership is reasonably strong. The leader is able to set the outcomes for the team and direct the team into achieving them. Trust and harmony exists between most team members. Workloads are shared while maintaining the status quo. They would be deemed, in performance reviews, to be 'doing their job'.

This team may stay together for some time: they like being in their comfort zone and are reluctant to change, grow or look at different opportunities.

The **_energetic team_** is collaborative: sharing ideas and supporting each other. Team members feel trusted, empowered to do their job and they do it well. They focus on working with others to achieve the best outcomes.

This team understands their purpose and direction and spends time focusing on the business and how they can keep improving, asking 'what if…?' questions to stretch their thinking.

The culture in the *dynamic team*, inspires people to come up with transformative ideas. Work just flows. Everyone feels valued, and there are high levels of trust between each member. Strengths and values are understood, and people know where they stand. Team members build on each other's capacity and learn together to create new ideas.

The whole team is invested in being the best they can be, individually and collectively, with a view to lifting the entire organisation. It goes beyond its KPIs and achieves amazing things. As well as having a high productive output, this team spends time building relationships, which is why trust is high. This team thinks strategically and drives both team, and organisational, success.

While the stress of a toxic team stifles creativity and strategic thinking, the environment of a dynamic team is invigorating, exciting and energising

This is the team we look forward to hanging out with every day; it's the team we learn from and who learns from us.

So how do we move from manic to magic, and become a team with high levels of trust, high performance, productivity and engagement? How do we create an environment that is energising and a fun place to be?

Shifting your team up the model is about changing how you communicate and how you relate to others. This book will help provide you with the confidence, understanding and tools to communicate effectively with others; to ensure that your conversations – no matter how difficult – generate positive outcomes for individuals and for the team.

It explains how to move from manic to magic; from a 'me and them' mindset to an 'us' mindset.

Section 1 discusses the need to understand 'me'. Until we understand who we are, what we value and what our strengths are, it's very hard to understand people around us. This section also covers identifying our desired state – where we want to be – and how to get there.

Section 2 focuses on the importance of 'them': that other person (or people) we need to build a relationship with. This is about being able to step into others' shoes, understand who they are and get a glimpse of how they think.

Section 3 is about how 'me' and 'them' come together to create 'us'. This is the magical space: a strong 'us' culture enables a team to be the best they can be.

PART I

ME

CHAPTER 1

Aware

Years ago, I worked with a leader who was skilful at building high-performing teams. I watched her build a team from scratch and the amazing results they achieved. Then, moving to a more senior role, she inherited a team that was barely functional. Again, I watched her work magic with this team, which became much more productive after several months.

I've always been curious about what makes someone good at creating performing teams and what I noticed was this leader was able to stay grounded. Being in touch with herself – understanding what she was feeling and why – meant that she could manage her emotional state and respond resourcefully if difficult situations arose. She had a good sense of her values, beliefs and strengths. Being self-aware meant that she connected easily with people: others would feel safe and free to be the best version of themselves.

When I look at successful leaders, time and again, it's their awareness of themselves that has given them the edge. Awareness of ourselves is about having a strong sense of who we are; we understand, and can predict, our emotional reactions to situations.

Conversely, when we are not conscious of our values and our strengths, we tend to be blind to what's going on, both within us and around us. We are more likely to misinterpret others; we react unconsciously, rather than consciously, often sending the wrong messages. This inevitably leads to less desirable outcomes, which undermines our confidence.

Fortunately self-awareness is something you can develop. Daniel Goleman describes how it can be strengthened in all of us. Increasing self-awareness starts with understanding who we are:

- our beliefs
- what we value
- our strengths and weaknesses
- our identity.

Knowing even a little more about each of these improves our ability to manage our emotions and be more flexible in the way we respond to situations.

If I know who I am, and I know who you are, then we can communicate better

Understanding what makes me tick and what makes you tick helps in all sorts of interactions we have: working together, negotiating, influencing, building high-performing teams.

Becoming self-aware is like getting new glasses: we have a clearer view of what's going on around us. There are different layers of self-awareness. Our values, beliefs, strengths and sense of self are like our essential character – they're what make us tick. But superimposed onto this are our emotions, which can change by the minute.

Tuning into our emotions is awareness at another level. Being aware of how we feel (and learning to manage this), gives us choice in how we interact with others, which helps us to create the best possible outcomes.

In our journey from manic to magic, understanding ourselves – how we are at the moment – is the first step. We may have a sense of where we'd like to get to but, just like finding the x on a treasure map, we need to figure out where we are in relation to it before we can work out how to get there.

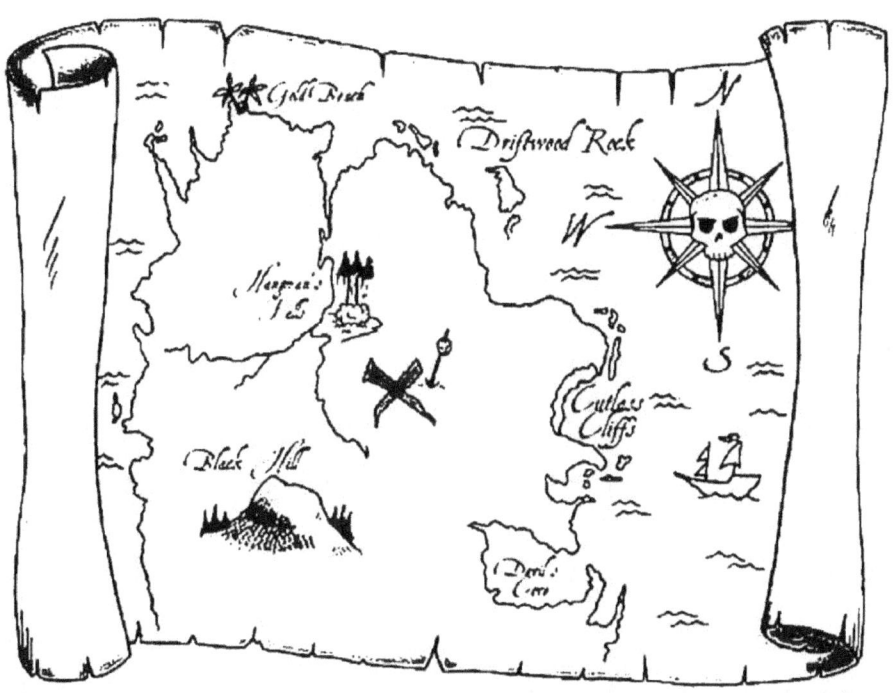

Now we need to get to know our present state: understanding our character and learning to habitually tune in to our emotional state.

Becoming aware of our present state

How can we become more aware of ourselves and others to improve the quality of our interactions?

Beliefs

> *"After many large engines refuse to pull a heavy train over a difficult hill, due to the impossible conditions, a smaller engine volunteers. Even though it seems laughable for this little engine to accomplish what the larger engines could not, the smaller engine proceeds to pull the train over the hill, while chanting, "I think I can, I think I can, I think I can."*

The little engine that could is all about the power of belief that whatever we believe becomes our reality.

We do not believe what we see; rather, we see what we already believe. For this reason, two people facing the same situation may interpret it differently, act according to their different beliefs, and experience different outcomes.

Our beliefs are assumptions we have about the world. They grow from what we see, hear, experience, read, or think about. They also grow from what we absorb from our parents, our family, our culture, and our childhood experiences. They are built as we go through life, so we tend not to question them. Once a belief is formed, we will work overtime to prove it right, even if the belief is something negative like 'nobody likes me' or 'I am a failure'.

> *"Beliefs have the power to create and the power to destroy."*
> *Anthony Robbins*

Beliefs fall into one of two overarching categories: empowering or limiting. Empowering beliefs help us make changes and decisions confidently.

Limiting beliefs do the exact opposite: they diminish our energy and can prevent us from changing or trying something new. We have an amazing ability to take any experience of our lives and create a meaning that disempowers us or one that can literally save our lives.

Limiting beliefs tend to be negative: 'I am not attractive, 'I will never be successful', 'I can't save money', or 'I can't work with those kind of people' are typical examples. Because they usually exist outside of our conscious awareness, we often recognise them as truths, rather than beliefs. Our beliefs are at the core of who we are. They govern us, even if they are harmful.

The great news is that beliefs can change. By identifying and understanding our beliefs, we can use them, or change them, to guide our decisions and behaviour in all areas of life. The more understanding and control we have over our beliefs, the more choice we present to ourselves.

Sometimes a belief may have been useful as a child, such as the belief instilled in many of us not talk to strangers. However, this is no longer useful for adults who need to build new connections (either for work or for relationships) with people we don't know. This belief doesn't serve us beyond a certain point in time and may become a limiting belief.

Limiting beliefs can be based on assumptions that are not true

The danger is that they can become true because they become our story. For instance, we may say 'I can't draw' or 'I'm not creative'. Because we believe we can't draw, we are afraid to try, or lose interest in developing our drawing skills, so our belief becomes self-fulfilling.

The reason I focus on limiting beliefs is to help people understand that they can change how they 'do' the world. Becoming aware of beliefs that may limit you or prevent you from achieving your desired state is often all that is needed to move on and achieve it.

Our limiting beliefs have a way of hiding from us – although we can often recognise other people's limiting beliefs through what they say, for example:

- 'I can't achieve my goal because of ….'
- 'My goal is achievable, but I don't have the ability to do it because ….'
- 'I don't deserve this because of … [something I am or am not, or something I have or have not done]."

Think about the way you say things to yourself or others. If you find yourself saying things like the examples above, ask yourself:

- Why is this goal unattainable?
- What skills do I need to develop to achieve this goal?
- Why don't I deserve to achieve this goal?

Continue to uncover the limiting beliefs that stand in the way of achieving a goal – you may find that one limiting belief leads to another, and then another. Keep digging and questioning to uncover those limiting beliefs that are preventing you from achieving your goals.

Limiting beliefs affect our behaviour, but once identified and dealt with they start to lose their power over us. Sometimes evidence that we can do something is all that is needed. Just try doing it. Once proven wrong, the belief will change instantly and lose its influence.

Think about a goal you have, that you're struggling to achieve. Consider what's stopping you from getting there.

The Coaching Session section at the end of this chapter provides prompting questions to identify your limiting beliefs.

Values

Values are a set of standards that determine our attitudes, choices and actions. They are like a compass that guides our lives, often functioning at an unconscious level, but guiding us nonetheless.

We all have an internalised system of values that we have developed throughout our lives – some that we may have developed independently, and some that we have inherited or absorbed from our families and culture.

Values are principles or qualities that we consider important, such as honesty, education, or hard work.

Our values reflect who we are, not what we would like to be

They are internal: they resonate with us and affect us at the deepest level. Every decision we make is based on our values, which we use as a guide to either avoid or aspire to something. Values influence why we do the things we do.

Understanding our value priorities can help lay important groundwork for making sound career decisions that fit our unique pattern of values, interests and talents. Work-related values underlie our choices about work. Some people value creativity; others place a premium on income or contribution.

When we honour our values, we find life is fulfilling, and it feels like it's in flow. When we don't honour our values, we can feel anxious. For example, if you value integrity and you are asked to cover up for a colleague at work, this will cause stress. You may not consciously be aware that it goes against one of your values, but you will sense the discomfort.

Workplaces are becoming more collaborative and people are increasingly looking not just for jobs, but also for organisations whose values and culture align with their own. By the same token, the most effective organisations attract people who already share most of their key values.

Identifying our values

In my last role I completed a value inventory (shown in Table 1) as my organisation was undergoing a major cultural change program.

At the time, I had been becoming increasingly unhappy and dissatisfied with my role and couldn't understand why, as I really liked my team. The role focussed on preparing marketing and communication material for a business unit and I had no, or very little interaction with stakeholders.

After completing the value inventory, I realised that a core value of mine is to be of service: to help people and have a customer focus. But this role gave me little opportunity to do so: it wasn't aligned with my values.

When we understand our values, change may need to occur

When what we do and the way we behave match our values, life and work is usually good. When these don't align with our values, we may feel unhappy and not know why.

In my case, I quit my job and created a role that was a better fit.

We all have more than one core value in our life. The values exercise in *the Coaching Session* at this end of this chapter will help you to identify your values.

Knowing our values makes it easier to us to make decisions as they offer a direction to travel in

Strengths

The realisation that my role didn't align with a core value (to be of service) was the beginning of a big change for me. My organisation's cultural change program also involved thousands of staff completing a 360-degree survey. A 360-degree survey is a questionnaire that an individual fills in, plus their manager, their team and peers and provides an overall view of that person's strengths and areas for development.

It was my first 360 and it showed that my job description didn't actually match what my responders and I agreed I was good at. There was very little in my role that I was good at. No wonder I wasn't having an enjoyable time. This light bulb moment became a beacon of change.

Even though, as a generalist, I am very good at finding parts of my job that I love, in this last role I was moving further and further away from what I was good at. The longer I stayed in the role, the more I started to doubt my strengths; I even began to wonder if I was good at anything.

Add in the lack of congruence with a core value, and it became clear that this role didn't give me the opportunity to be my best. I was just being average or worse!

I believe that if we are able to use our strengths, we will love what we do. In contrast, we are unlikely to enjoy doing something that we aren't particularly good at and find difficult to complete. Are you using your strengths in your current role?

Academics such as Dr Martin Seligman and Dr Christopher Peterson found that people have several times more potential for growth when they invest energy in developing their strengths instead of only correcting their weaknesses.

But it can be challenging to work out what our strengths are. One way is to ask people close to us. Often our strengths are revealed when we think about our accomplishments, moments of pride, and great performance.

What event in your life characterises you at your very best?

At first, we may only have a general awareness of each strength – being great with people, for example. Try to dig deeper: in what way are you great with people? Are you empathetic and compassionate? Able to have difficult conversations? Or perhaps good at providing direction? The more defined our strengths are the more we are able to leverage them.

There are also tools and questionnaires available for identifying strengths. The VIA Survey of Character Strengths is a free online self-assessment that provides information to help us understand our core characteristics and best qualities. I have used this tool for many years to provide my clients with an easy way to identify their strengths.

Another great resource is the book *Strengths Finder 2.0* by Tom Rath and an online survey, available for a fee.

If you can work to your strengths, you're more likely to infuse your work with meaning and passion and have more impact

Emotions

Being able to tune into our emotions is a crucial element of self-awareness. Daniel Goleman, author of *Emotional Intelligence*, puts it this way:

> *Self-awareness relates to our ability to understand our personal moods, emotions and drives, as well as their effect on others. High self-awareness creates self-confidence, the ability to self-assess, and the ability to laugh at ourselves. When we are self-aware, we monitor our emotional state and can correctly identify and name our emotions. We have a strong understanding of who we are.*

We are more effective when we are conscious of our moods and feelings, and aware of how they influence both our own thoughts and decisions, and those of the people around us.

People who are able to express how they feel are often described as genuine and trustworthy; they're usually able to engage more effectively with others. Expressing emotions helps to create greater understanding with our team and colleagues.

One way to increase our self-awareness is to tune into our emotions consciously; to check our current emotional state and the reasons behind what we are feeling.

The following questions are useful:

- Was a particular emotion triggered by what someone said or something that happened?
- How long do these emotions last and what sort of intensity are they?

Are these emotions useful to lead effectively?

Awareness of our emotions creates resilience during stressful times, allows us to cope more effectively with work demands, and improves workplace productivity and performance. We can practise tuning in to our emotions by keeping track of them for a day.

Identifying our desired state

Once we are more familiar with our current state, who we are, what and why we are doing what we are doing, we are in a better position to identify where we want to end up – our desired state – and how we might get there.

I wrote about the 'present to desired state' method in my first book, *The XX Project*, and feedback from readers confirmed how important it is to spend time working on where we want to get to.

Having read this far, you have a sense of where you are currently (your present state): you have a better understanding of your beliefs (including those that may be limiting you), your strengths and your important values.

Being aware of our beliefs, values, strengths and emotions becomes easier and easier the more we practise. It's a bit like driving a car. When we learn to drive, at first it takes a lot of time and effort. It feels like we need to pay attention to every little detail, be aware of everything going on around us. We can feel overwhelmed and exhausted after every drive. But as we become accustomed to driving it becomes easier and requires less conscious attention.

Eventually, we drive without even thinking and manage to get where we want to go safely, without having to work too hard. We remember the awkwardness of those initial steps, but now we 'know' how to drive we don't give it a second thought. In the same way, self-awareness becomes second nature as we continue to practise.

Now it is time to turn our attention to the future: our desired state.

Imagine arriving in Melbourne on a plane. We're are waiting in the taxi rank at Melbourne Airport and finally a taxi is in front of us. We get in and the driver says, 'Where to?'

What would happen if we said, 'I don't want to go to Bendigo, I don't want to go to Brunswick, and I don't want to go to Brighton'? What does the taxi driver do? Nothing. She has no idea where to take us.

This happens in life: we often know what we *don't* want to do, or what we *don't* want; however, we may be less clear on where we *do* want to go or what we *do* want.

Present to desired state ('P to D') is a method that helps us get to where we want to be.

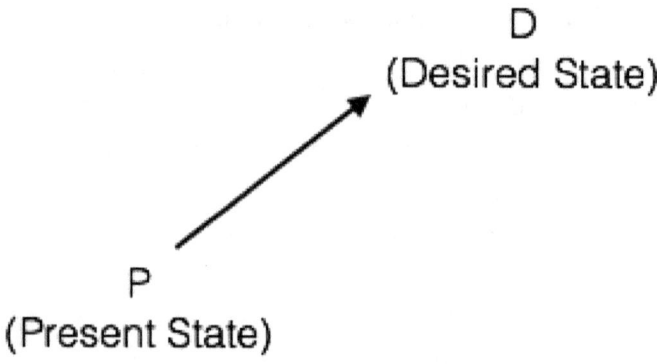

Figure 2: Present to Desired State

Identifying our desired state is about creating a well-formed outcome. The term 'well-formed outcome' is a process originally developed by John Grinder & Richard Bandler and is about developing a quality outcome that is more than a vague wish or goal.

Any goal or desired state, big or small, can be turned into a well-formed outcome. If several steps are needed for us to move from our present state to our desired state, we can use well-formed outcomes at each one.

It's ultimately up to us and no-one else to create and achieve our own well-formed outcome. A coach, mentor, friend, or colleague can help us through the process, but we have to do the work ourselves.

Use *the Coaching Session* at this end of this chapter to create a well-formed outcome.

Your personal coaching session

Limiting Beliefs

Questions to help identify and change limiting beliefs include:

- What beliefs are preventing you from achieving your goal?
- Where do you think these beliefs stem from? (Think about major events in your life and what beliefs may have been formed).
- Consider one of your limiting beliefs. What would you need to do to remove or diminish this limiting belief and create a more empowering one?
- What are some empowering beliefs that will help you reach your goal?

Your Values

This values exercise is a useful way to discover the relative importance of each of our values.

1. Start by asking, 'What is important in my life?' Then continue: 'What else is important in my life?' You can use the words on in Table 1 as prompts. Underline those that are most important.
2. Narrow down the list and circle the top eight values that are absolutely essential to satisfy you in your work and life.
3. Chunk words together or clarify meaning for yourself, as some values may be similar.
4. Rank your eight important values by asking, 'Is 1 more important than 2?' 'Is 1 more important than 3?', and so on. Put a mark against the value that is most important.
5. Now write out the top values and define what they mean to you.

To help you with this, think about your key life decisions. It could be when you changed jobs, moved to a new house, or started or left a relationship.

In reflecting on these key moments, consider which values were being either honoured or not at that point. Consider the values that fuelled the decision-making. You may be surprised when you compare your values this way. Values you may have thought were very important might be further down your hierarchy than you first realised.

The following questions may also help to clarify your values:

- What must you have in your life to feel fulfilled?
- What are the values you absolutely must honour – or a part of you dies?
- What values do you see in your own life?
- What values do you sell out on first?
- Where do your values show up?
- Which values are sometimes neglected?
- Where are you too flexible?
- What value is being stretched a bit too much?
- What are your wants versus your musts?
- Where are you an automatic yes or no?
- Where do you limit yourself?
- If you didn't limit yourself, what might you do? (What value would that uphold?)
- Where are you too comfortable?
- What are you willing to risk?
- What will free you up?

Having identified your values, keep these front and centre in your mind: they become your guide when deciding which activities are worthwhile committing to and being interested in.

Fairness	Flexibility	Teamwork	Integrity
Competence	Environment	Leadership	Prestige
Mastery	Choice	Caring	Achievement
Risk taking	Security	Competition	Respect
Early adoption	High earnings	Cooperation	Responsibility
Attention to detail	Taking action	Diversity	Power
Social activism	Structure	Collaboration	Influence
Learning	Being easy-going	Humour	Appreciation
Excellence	Being calm	Harmony	Helping
Focus	Quiet	Autonomy	Belonging
Creativity	Order	Recognition	Community
Variety	Excitement	Support	Equality
Growth	Pressure	Trust	Independence
Knowledge	Predictability	People contact	Contribution
Control	Location	Independence	Service
Adventure	Public contact	Fun	Authenticity
Curiosity	Status	Balance	Commitment
Initiative	Honesty	Having impact	Balance
Cultural identity	Punctuality	Open communication	Health

Table 1: Values Inventory

Emotions

Here's an exercise to try: Write down what you are feeling every hour or so. At the end of the day, review how your emotions fluctuated across the day. Identify the points when your mood shifted and work out what happened to cause the shift.

Creating a Well-Formed Outcome

The questions below form the basis for creating a well-formed outcome.

1. What do you want to achieve? This must be stated in the positive (what you do want, not what you don't want).
2. Is it achievable? Has this ever been done before?
3. Is achieving this outcome under your control? The outcome must be able to be self-initiated and self-maintained (i.e. you don't need other people to help you achieve it).
4. Use sensory language to describe how you will experience achieving this goal, which you can accept as evidence that you have achieved it.
    a. What do you see? Close your eyes and imagine that the outcome has been reached. What are you seeing around you, what are you doing, and what are other people doing?
    b. What can you hear? What are other people saying and what are you saying to yourself?
    c. What are you feeling?
    d. What can you taste or smell?
5. For what purpose do you want to achieve this outcome? Start your answer with '*so that…*' Keep repeating this question until you really reach the highest and best purpose for achieving this well-formed outcome.
6. Are the costs and consequences of achieving this outcome, including the time involved, acceptable to you and anyone else affected by it? For example, will there be any issues with friends' expectations of the way you are now, compared to how you will be when you achieve this?
7. If you could have this outcome now, would you take it?
8. What resources do you need to achieve this (tangible and intangible)?

9. What is the first step in achieving this goal? Is the first step achievable? What's the first thing you can do?

This is a structured way to define where we are currently and where we want to get to, and to quiet down that voice inside that may be expressing our deepest concerns and fears.

Having a tangible first step to achieving a goal and acting on it will usually start the process going. Once the first step is identified and achieved, it's about working out what the step is after that and then after that.

Use this process to create a well-formed outcome for yourself. Start with something simple that you want to achieve in the short term.

CHAPTER 2

Adapt

Quite a few years ago I shared a puzzle I'd found with my team. It was just before a long weekend and when I sat down to work it out I realised that based on its instructions, it appeared incomplete so I decided it could not be solved and promptly forgot about it.

When a team member emailed me an answer, I realised that I had developed a limiting belief. I spent the next few hours working through the puzzle (and creating a couple of spreadsheets) and came up with the same answer as my colleague!

In creating this false and limiting belief, I had become closed to other ways of thinking. Dr Carol S. Dweck, author of *Mindset*, calls this a 'closed mindset'. In contrast, an 'open' or 'growth mindset' is a mind that is open to possibilities. An open mindset is behaviourally flexible: able to consider other options and be adaptive. We can actually shift between open and closed mindsets depending on context.

After the weekend I gave the puzzle to my teenage children to try. They completed it in 10 minutes, in their heads! Sheesh!

Our ability to adapt to what's going on around us is known as behavioural flexibility. The person with the most flexibility of thought, feeling, language and behaviour always has the edge over others. This is discussed in more detail in Chapter 5.

We can be either behaviourally flexible or inflexible. An open mindset enables us to be more flexible, meaning we adapt more easily to different situations. An open mindset is especially beneficial, then, when we are experiencing change, either in our workplace or in our lives.

Being able to adapt is crucial, if we are to reach our desired state. On this journey, we will need to step outside our comfort zone, recognise what keeps us stuck in the present, and take responsibility for our actions.

Moving out of our comfort zone

Early in my career I took no initiative in shaping my future. I felt like my life was being shaped by external events and people, rather than by me, and eventually came to the realisation that my career choices (or lack thereof) were harming my strengths, skills and happiness.

I needed to be able to move out of my comfort zone, face my fears and focus on my strengths and what I loved to do. I also needed to stop blaming other people, things, and circumstances for where I was in life.

Most people are very familiar with their comfort zone. It's where we are doing the same old stuff: we know the people we work with, we may have had the same desk for some time, we are familiar with our surroundings, the work we do is pretty much the same day-to-day, and we are not learning anything new. Our comfort zone has certainty – something we crave – and we tend to stay there at any cost.

We can go through life denying that we have to do something, blaming someone or something else, or justifying our actions – perhaps not even aware we are doing so – in order to avoid being confronted by uncomfortable truths. However, this can make us a victim of external forces, rather than an agent of our own destiny.

The trouble with staying in our comfort zone is that the states of certainty, closure and confidence that we experience there shut down our curiosity and leads to a closed mindset.

When we are out of our comfort zone we may feel:

- anxious

- uncomfortable
- afraid
- out-of-control
- frustrated
- excited
- exhilarated.

We may experience physical responses such as an increased heart rate, sweaty palms, or a knot in the pit of our stomach. We perceive these as negative – to be avoided.

So why would we want to go there?

Think back to the first time you drove a car. Did you experience any of these physical reactions? You may have been very anxious. With time, you probably overcame those feelings and can now drive calmly, effortlessly, and skilfully without even thinking.

This suggests that being outside the comfort zone has some relationship to learning new things. By definition, the comfort zone consists of things we know – which means we can't learn something new from within it. The zone outside our comfort zone is called the 'learning zone'.

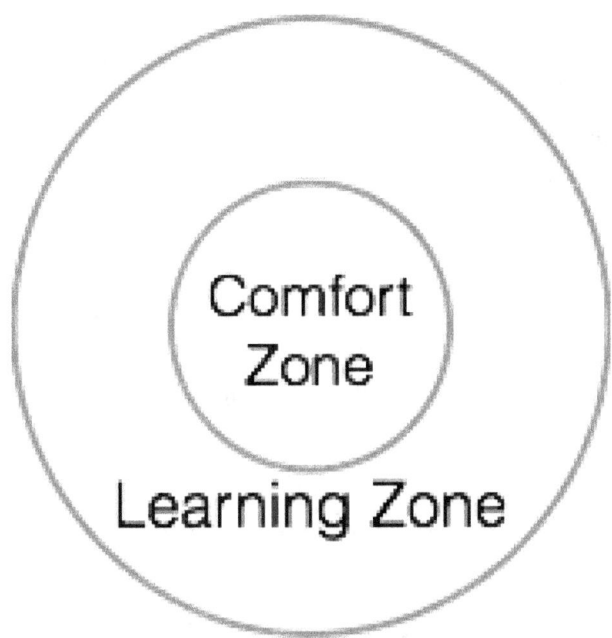

Figure 3. Comfort Zone / Learning Zone

Moving out our comfort zone can feel like jumping out of a plane and hoping the parachute works. Nevertheless, if we never leave it, we can't learn and grow, and we could become bored and complacent.

How much we want something, or want to change something, relates directly to our willingness to feel the discomfort of the learning zone and stay with it until it becomes comfortable and familiar. The more we do something uncomfortable, the more comfortable we become with it, and the more our comfort zone grows.

Do you know anyone who stays in their comfort zone? When a new idea is suggested, or they are asked to do something different, they may respond with things like:

- 'That would never work.'
- 'That's not how it's done.'
- 'I could never do that.'
- 'I haven't been trained to do that.'
- 'It's not in my job description.'

I have become familiar with many excuses to avoid discomfort in my work helping people develop their public speaking skills. (This perhaps isn't surprising considering the fear of speaking in public is often rated ahead of the fear of dying.) Common avoidance strategies I hear are:

- 'I don't need to know how to do that.' (denying the need to learn)
- 'My manager made me…' (blaming someone else)
- 'This isn't part of my job description.' (justifying why you can't do something).

Lateness is another classic. 'I'm late because of the traffic.' 'I'm late because of the trains.' I understand that you can't control the traffic and you can't control the trains. The question is: what can we control? We can listen to traffic reports, control the time we leave, or choose how to travel.

Once we start picking ourselves up on this we find that we run out of excuses. My colleagues refer to these strategies for avoidance as 'DBJs':

- Deny
- Blame
- Justify

Catching the DBJs

Think of something you have always wanted to do and haven't got around to. What are your DBJs? They might include 'I don't have time', 'I can't afford it', 'I'm not skilled enough to do it', 'my family wouldn't approve', 'it's too expensive', or 'I don't really want to do that anyway'.

When we are *denying, blaming* or *justifying,* we are playing the victim

How can we move from being a victim to a learner?

When we catch ourselves in denial, the best response is to add 'yet' or 'at this point in time' to our statement. For example, 'I'm not skilled enough to do it *yet*'; 'I can't do that *at this point in time*'.

When we catch ourselves blaming, the best response is to ask ourselves, 'What is my 50%?' In any interaction or situation, we are involved in, we contribute at least 50% to the outcome. For example, during an argument with someone it's easy to blame the other person for being bad tempered or mean. The question is, 'How did I contribute to the upset – what is my 50%?' We shoulder 50% of any conversation we are part of with another person.

When we catch ourselves justifying, it is also useful to consider our 50%. In the example 'I'm late because of the traffic', it's easy to justify why we were late – the road conditions, other drivers, poor city planning, traffic lights, and so on. The question is what percentage we want to give to these. This is not about traffic, it's about being late and our part in that. What is our 50%?

Dumping the excuses

Thinking in these terms moves us from DBJing to ARAing: accepting, taking responsibility and being accountable.

Instead of denying that we can achieve something, we *accept* our own actions.

Instead of blaming something or someone, we *take responsibility* for our own actions.

Instead of justifying why we did or didn't do something, we are *accountable* for our actions.

Ask ourselves the question, 'What if the opposite were true?' In the example 'this isn't part of my job description', ask 'what if the opposite was true and this was part of my job description?' It doesn't change the facts; however, it does create a shift in our mindset and can open up different possibilities. This is often enough to shift our perspective and create some change in what we are, or are not, doing.

The power of these techniques was brought home to me recently with a client, Susan, who had wanted to achieve some big goals but kept finding that they just weren't happening for one reason or another.

Susan had joined my leadership coaching program to focus on her career, but two personal goals came up over the course of our coaching engagement. She had been procrastinating about these for years. She wanted to get fit and lose some weight.

As I mentioned earlier, we will try to stay in our comfort zone. Susan was being a victim. There were lots of reasons why she wasn't achieving her personal goals: her husband didn't support her with achieving them, the timing wasn't right, it was too soon after Christmas, it was too close to Easter, it was winter, it was summer… On and on it went.

Susan needed to move from the 'deny, blame, justify' strategy to the 'accept, take responsibility, be accountable' strategy: accept that it was up to her, and be accountable for her own action (or inaction). She had to move from being a victim and step into her learning zone.

Once she understood the comfort-zone concept and the fear we experience moving into our learning zone, she was able to make some changes.

She worked through the steps to create a well-formed outcome and realised that she hadn't fully articulated the consequences of becoming fit and losing some weight. She needed to assume all responsibility for achieving this outcome, including the time involved.

Susan decided to commit to action by joining a gym and hiring a personal trainer. She also tweaked her diet so it didn't disrupt family cooking and meals, and focused on what she was eating without having to rely on her husband and family supporting her.

She found it confronting at first and, at times, difficult. However, by facing her excuses, inaction, and victim strategies, and owning her actions and their consequences, change started to happen. Susan allowed herself to be uncomfortable and move out of her comfort zone.

And the last time I checked she had a scheduled exercise regime maintaining her fitness levels and sustaining her ideal weight.

- Get out of your comfort zone.

- Stop DBJing start ARAing.
- Accept that it's up to you, become responsible for your own actions and accountable for your life.

Making small improvements every day (self-edit)

Do you ever have days where you wish you could hit replay and do things differently?' While we can't travel back in time, we can relive that day in our minds and imagine how we could have acted differently for a better outcome.

A technique called a self-edit is a self-awareness tool that helps us improve our performance using feedback and correction. Using this technique, our behaviour can become more flexible. We change and adapt to our circumstances.

Using the self-edit technique daily helps us to become more aware of our DBJs and turn them into ARAs.

Self-Edit (memory management to enhance performance)

We review our day as it occurred, noting all the areas that didn't go so well, then review the day again and imagine it running seamlessly with great interactions. The next time this interaction occurs, in our mind we will have already responded differently.

We can select areas from our everyday life that we wish to capitalise on, as well as things we wish to change.

We get the opportunity to rerun our day (or week, or month). We cannot change how others responded, but we can review how we responded and mentally adjust how we could have responded emotionally and behaviourally.

Mistakes are not learning experiences unless we learn from them

Self-editing is a tool that converts mistakes into learning experiences. When we adjust our attention to become more aware during a self-edit, we avoid the circular thinking that keeps us revisiting moments of pain, shame or embarrassment.

Use *the Coaching Session* at this end of this chapter to learn more about Self-editing.

Your personal coaching session

<u>Self-edit method</u>

1. Run through the chosen time period (for example, a day), paying special attention to those events that didn't turn out as you would have liked.
2. Run through the time period again, this time constructing how the events could have played out if your behaviour had been different.
3. Lock these changes in by running through the time period again, as if it had gone seamlessly.
4. Now think of a time in the future where a similar scenario is likely to occur. Imagine it running in the same seamless way as in Step 3.

As a new habit, each night before going to sleep, we can review our day and think about different ways we could have responded to events. This way we will can build up our behavioural flexibility and begin to respond and adapt more appropriately to the world around us.

CHAPTER 3

Commit

My first career was in nursing. After graduating as a registered nurse, I took time off for a break from shift work and landed a role as receptionist in a leasing firm and ended up managing a prestige motor vehicle leasing portfolio. This was a huge learning curve that hooked me into the world of finance. It was pure luck that I landed that role.

This pattern would continue for much of my career: rather than making conscious career choices, I was swept from one position to the next like driftwood on the tide.

Our leasing firm was taken over by an international bank and the mining director needed an assistant to create and run a syndicated lending agency division. Again, by luck, I was appointed and experienced another huge learning curve.

From there I joined a major Australian bank and won the role largely due to my name. The team leader had asked the recruiter to 'find another Marie' – someone with the same skills as a Marie already in her team. Coincidence?

I came to realise that I was a generalist and reasonably good at doing most things. Even if the job wasn't very interesting or challenging I could always find something about it that I loved.

For my entire career, I had gone with the flow, taken roles that others had suggested, and mostly enjoyed them. But I finally ended up in a role that didn't play to any of my strengths and, for the first time, didn't look forward to coming to work each day.

That was when I became committed to my personal development journey. I gained a new perspective on what I was good at and what I should be doing and the best careers to achieve that.

An opportunity for redundancy was the catalyst to leave and start my coaching business. I needed to move out of my comfort zone, face my fears and start focusing on my strengths and what I loved to do.

It was the first career move where I directly controlled my direction. This time, it wasn't by good luck; it was by good management – specifically:

- I recognised where I wanted to be - self-awareness
- I was prepared to move out of my comfort zone to get there - having an open mindset
- I understood my 'why'
- I was ready to own my choice - being accountable.

This process applies whether you are changing careers, as I was, or changing something about how you operate, which we'll discuss further in the next section.

Making the change

Committing to something starts with understanding where we want to get to. We all have moments of choice in life, like I did with the bank, where we need to decide: this direction or that direction? There are many of these moments but, especially if we are not self-aware, we often miss them.

Having worked with leaders and teams for many years, I know many individuals are stagnating in their roles and not even really aware of the fact. They just know that work is 'difficult', 'not enjoyable', and in some cases 'toxic'.

Developing greater awareness of ourselves – who we are, what's important to us (our values) and what we're good at (our strengths) – enables us to recognise what we should be doing. It helps us to identify where we want to be – which means that we are more likely to make informed, appropriate choices when the opportunity arises.

Having an open mindset allows us to consider possibilities and see the benefits of moving outside our comfort zone (into our learning zone) to pursue a direction that is likely to benefit us.

Unless we take the time to define our direction and strategy, we can't ultimately grow. If we don't know where we want to go, or how we want to grow; if we don't develop a plan to get there, our intentions don't really matter. Without a direction and strategy, we are unlikely to evolve; instead we'll merely substitute one ill-suited activity for another.

Once we have determined our desired state, it's then about owning our decision and holding ourselves accountable to pursue it

That means identifying the first step to achieve our well-formed outcome and completing it. And then when that is achieved, identifying the next step and then the next. How we hold ourselves accountable takes many different guises. It could be just deciding and then doing the work; it could be telling someone else and asking them to hold us accountable; or, it could be setting up some reward for achieving that first step.

Actually committing to a change – be it a change in career, or to a new way of operating – inevitably means moving outside our comfort zone. It's challenging! So how can we make that leap?

Being clear on the reasons *why* we want to move in this particular direction or make this change, being in touch with our vision, helps us commit. Committing is the act of putting a stake in the ground and standing by our decision – owning our choice.

Bringing it together

The 'Me' section has focused on the strategies we can use to make an intentional and well-chosen change from an unsatisfactory situation.

It starts with understanding our character – what makes us tick – and how that fits with where we are currently. This gives us an informed position from which to identify our desired state.

Committing to our desired state means stepping out of our comfort zone, catching our DBJs and switching to a strategy of accepting, taking responsibility, and being accountable for our actions.

We need an open mindset in order to change. It also helps to be behaviourally flexible. We can become more flexible in our behaviour with practice. The self-edit is a technique where rehearsing alternative responses to a situation in our minds improves our flexibility in responding to future events.

Our journey towards our desired state may start with a very small step. The well-formed outcome method provides structure to guide us in choosing an appropriate goal, and achieving it.

My journey of self-development started with becoming more self-aware. I came to understand my values and strengths and realised that I hadn't made conscious career choices. This knowledge helped me to identify where I wanted to get to, which was to start my own business as a coach. This would mean moving out of my comfort zone and stepping into my learning zone.

I discovered that I loved learning; but found that along the way I often wanted to step back into my comfort zone – and a range of DBJs encouraged me to do just that.

Some of my DBJs in my business involved my belief that I sucked at selling, particularly selling myself and my products; I had a range of justifications for why I couldn't sell – such as: people didn't have time to meet with me; the people I met with weren't the decision makers; I didn't want to be seen as pushy so couldn't ask them to buy. On and on it went, so I could stay in my comfort zone and not sell.

Moving to my learning zone meant that:

- I had to accept that I did have to sell if I wanted a business.
- I had to take responsibility for selling and not wish someone else would do it for me. I completed some training programs to build my sales muscle.
- I created a range of strategies to hold myself accountable for selling. Things like a visual (and large) sales funnel on my wall tracking contacts, meetings and sales, and setting up a customer relationship management system (CRM) to create tasks to be completed at specific times.

While this section has focused on the individual – who you are, your strengths, values and your desired state – it can be applied equally to teams.

As team leader, it's valuable to consider the teams strengths, values and beliefs. Where is your team on the manic-to-magic model? What is the vision for the team?

If you feel the team is in the bottom half of the manic-to-magic model (toxic, frantic or erratic), how can you move it towards the top (authentic, energic or dynamic)?

Is the team in their comfort zone and not challenging their thinking? When pushed, does it resort to DBJs to stay there? How can they turn these into ARAs? How can you safely move them into their learning zone, willing to experiment and try new ideas?

PART 2

THEM

THEM

Have you ever spent time with someone who makes you feel that they really see you and really hear you?

A mate of mine, Mike, grew up with profoundly deaf parents, which meant that to be able to communicate with them he needed to focus completely on them, watching them to make sure he understood what they were signing, and that they understood him.

When I first met him, I was initially taken aback by the deep attention Mike focussed on me when we were talking. His attention had a laser focus and I felt like I was in a spotlight. The depth of his awareness and listening skill is extraordinary. It is a joy to spend time with someone who is able to focus completely on the person they are conversing with.

This kind of awareness of others builds trust. It allows conversations to flow in all sorts of areas, and new thinking to emerge. The same does not happen with people of low awareness.

CHAPTER 4

Engage

Focusing on engaging with others and building great relationships with our team members is key to creating high-performing teams. When we are in a work environment that is enjoyable, with open and trusting communication our work feels more rewarding and less stressful.

In the 'Me' section I discussed the importance of increasing our own self-awareness in order to become more intentional about our behaviour, our interactions and our choices. Self-awareness is only part of the equation: awareness of others is equally important when it comes to building strong, productive relationships.

Having either low self-awareness or low awareness of others can compromise our relationships and our performance, as is demonstrated in the awareness model (Figure 4).

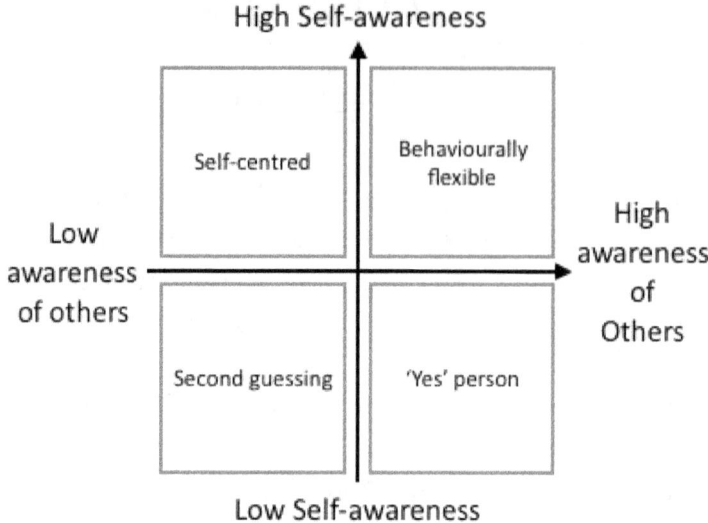

Figure 4: Awareness model

If we have high self-awareness with low awareness of others we can be self-centred. We focus on us and our feelings, not seeing our impact on others. We are usually not aware of how what we've said or done affects others – or we don't care.

If we have low self-awareness and high awareness of others we can be a 'yes' person. Others may see us as not able to think for ourselves, or always changing our mind depending on whom we last spoke with.

If we have low self-awareness and low awareness of others we are always second guessing ourselves. Should we do that or not? Should we involve others? We flip flop around, basing decisions on what we think, then what others think, and ultimately don't come to any sort of conclusion.

When we have high self-awareness plus high awareness of others, we are able to be behaviourally flexible. We are able to step into other people's shoes and see where they are, then filter these different perspectives with who we are.

Awareness of others

Having awareness of others is something we can become better at: it's a learnable skill. We can start by listening and really working to understand the meaning of people's words.

In his book *Deep Listening*, Oscar Trimboli says that awareness is about how we listen. It's about listening to others: listening for what's being said and listening for what's not being said. It's a full body experience. Awareness is opening up our radar, to allow us to gather more data and then use that productively.

I sometimes use an activity in workshops where I ask people to pair up and share a story about moment in their life that means something to them. Afterwards, their partner is asked to identify the underlying point and work out what they are passionate about.

I share a story about the time I had to care for my sons' lizards (bearded dragons) while the boys went away with their Father over Easter.

Now I hate handling lizards or anything scaly but felt that I could manage this. Except that, on the day they left, one lizard's leg was badly bitten by a larger lizard and required veterinary attention. This meant a one hour drive to a lizard specialist and then antibiotics every four hours, which required me to hold the lizard in one hand while trying to stick a syringe in its mouth. The good news is that the lizard and its leg survived.

When I ask the people in the workshop what I am passionate about they usually correctly identify that I am passionate about my children and will do pretty much anything for them, including holding a lizard multiple times a day. Listening deeply allows us to tap into more than just the words the other person is saying.

When was the last time you listened to someone to really understand what they were saying – not to judge, or confirm what you were already thinking, or reject what they were saying – but really listened to their words, watched their body language and developed an awareness of them?

We all love the feeling of connection with others and acceptance, and dislike feeling judged or criticised.

When was the last time you focused on someone to the extent that you picked up on what they were thinking, or what wasn't being said, and maybe recognised what they wanted to explore further with you?

Listening deeply builds our understanding of others.

Perceptual Positions

They say you can't really understand another person's experience until you've walked a mile in their shoes – or, in other words, imagined the world from their perspective.

Perceptual positions is a technique to increase our awareness of ourselves and others and used three perspectives or points of view. In first position, we look at the world through our own eyes, hear with our own ears, and feel, taste and smell using our own senses. Our own point of view, beliefs, and assumptions influence our perspective.

In second position, we try to imagine being in the other person's shoes – experiencing what they may be feeling and seeing. Matching the other's breathing, posture and voice helps us to imagine their point of view, beliefs and assumptions, and see the world through their eyes. We may even look back at ourselves in first position and see ourselves from the other person's perspective.

In third position, we act as an observer, watching what is happening, and possibly forming opinions about the subjects of observation (first and second positions). We are dissociated from both ourselves and the other person, simply observing the interactions of these two people. In third position, we are like a fly on the wall watching the interaction between two people.

We can often spend our lives inhabiting one perceptual position (and not necessarily first position), which limits our understanding and therefore our flexibility in interacting with others. Being able to switch points of view and consider multiple perspectives gives us much greater insight into a situation or interaction.

With practice we can learn to live in first position as our home base and move to third and second position to understand more in our interactions with others.

Understanding and being able to move through different perceptual positions helps us to build great relationships. We become aware of things that, if we lived in one position only, we may never notice. We may become aware of our tone of voice, or our body language when we observe from second or third position and may realise that is not how we want to be seen or heard. That awareness allows us to adjust how we are being; to become more flexible in our behaviour.

I use a perceptual positions activity in workshops. Participants are asked to think about a recent conversation they have had which could have gone better and then experience the conversation from each position.

When they have completed exercise, I ask what they noticed. Typically, I hear comments like: 'I wasn't aware I stood like that, I appear closed off'; 'I would have a different conversation now if I could have it again'; 'I have a better idea of how the other person was feeling; as an observer watching those two people I felt there was a complete disconnect and misunderstanding of what was being said'.

Refer to *the Coaching Session* at the end of this chapter to learn how the move between perceptual positions.

Jumping to conclusions

Are you someone who tends to make assumptions about other people quickly? Have you ever had 'aha!' moments where you changed your belief about someone after learning something new?

Jumping to conclusions can compromise our ability to engage with others. The Ladder of Inference is a model created by organisational psychologist and former professor at Harvard Business School Chris Argyris.

The model shows how we reach conclusions and build beliefs. It's a tool that helps us understand how we can jump to the wrong conclusions and enables us to consider other points of view.

The ladder describes our thinking process to get from a fact to a decision or an action and how beliefs are created.

At the bottom of the ladder we are exposed to billions of bits of observable data which we are physically unable to process. As we move up the ladder, based on our beliefs and prior experiences we select data (at an unconscious level), add meaning to our selection, make assumptions about that meaning to reach conclusions. This leads to us building a belief, or reinforcing a belief we have, and we act accordingly.

For instance, I may be chairing a meeting and notice Mary arrive 15 minutes late. Starting at the bottom of the ladder, I select data that Mary is late. I add meaning to that: 'the last time I chaired this meeting Mary was also late'.

I make assumptions about that meaning: 'Mary doesn't respect me and she is trying to disrupt my meeting'. I conclude that there is nothing I can do to salvage this relationship and build a belief that Mary does not support me.

I will then select the data to reinforce that belief and act accordingly.

Bob is also in the meeting, and notices Mary arrive, and he selects different data that Mary 'sits next to the boss'. Bob goes up his ladder and adds meaning and assumptions around the fact the Mary is after a promotion and therefore schmoozing the boss. Bob's belief is that, though he also wanted that promotion, there's no point in him trying because Mary will probably win out. He will then look for and select data to support that belief.

And so it goes: everyone will select different data, reach different conclusions and build beliefs about Mary.

Rather than acting on my beliefs and looking for data to support them, I should be looking for different data or checking that I have added the right meaning to the data I've selected. Instead of building a belief that Mary doesn't like me, I could catch up with Mary after the meeting to discuss her lateness. 'Hi Mary, I noticed that you came in late to the meeting and I realised that you were also late the last time I chaired this meeting. Can you tell me about that?'

Mary could respond with: 'Oh, I'm so sorry, every fourth Monday I have to take my father to an appointment which means I get to work 30 minutes later than normal – that must correspond with the last two times you've chaired the meeting. I should have realised and told you.'

Belief busted!

Bob could also follow up with Mary to get some more data about his belief. Imagine if she said, 'I had to sit next to the boss, as that was the only seat left!'

Pausing, reflecting and finding more data is crucial to breaking this cycle where our conclusions build beliefs, which in turn influence what data we select, so we filter out other information that might lead us to alternative conclusions.

As leaders, the need for openness and transparency is crucial to building great leadership capabilities and developing high performing teams. Without information, we are prone to filling in the gaps, making our own meanings and building beliefs based on insufficient data.

Awareness of the Ladder of Inference helps us to reach better conclusions and make sense of other's interpretations. It can also assist us to discuss how we may have each have come to see things differently.

If we are challenging someone else's assumptions, we need to consider how to do this without creating conflict, so we can reach shared conclusions with each other.

Think about:

- How have I reached this conclusion and is it the right conclusion?
- Why am I making these assumptions?
- Do I have enough facts to support my belief?
- What has led someone else to believe something different?

The meaning of what I say is what you understand

We assume that our meaning is clear when we say something. But your interpretation of my words may not match mine. If I give you a word and ask you for its meaning, your answer will likely be different to the person next to you. For example, lock in the first thought that comes to mind when you see the word 'circus'.

What was it? Did you see a picture of something? A circus tent? An elephant? Or maybe the ringmaster inside the tent? Was it the word 'circus' inside your mind? Maybe you smelt something associated with circus – the sawdust in the ring, or the smell of elephant poo! Maybe you heard circus music.

If I ask a group to do this activity, everyone will usually have a different response. I could ask the same question for the word 'success'. We would find that there are many different responses to the meaning of success.

This has implications for our teams. Suppose, in a team meeting, I say that we need to focus on success. Unless I define what I mean everyone might have a different understanding of what we are aiming for. I may mean meeting KPIs; someone else may assume success means leaving on time every day; someone else may think it means delivering a project on time.

It's easy to mistakenly assume that we are talking about the same thing. In fact, a Stanford University study found that nine out of ten conversations miss the mark. It's an alarming thought!

To make sure more of our conversations hit the mark, we have to really listen to understand what people are saying. That means checking in to make sure that we've interpreted correctly, confirming that we have the same understanding. We might ask questions such as:

- Tell me more about that…
- How do you define …?
- What does this mean to you?
- What does it look like when you do that?
- So …
- What is another way of looking at this?
- Can you explain that another way?
- How might someone else describe this?

It's like an archaeologist digging down layer by layer and increasing their understanding with each new artefact. We need to learn how to dig out the meaning of what people are saying.

The power of words

Just as we may not realise that our interpretation differs from someone else's, we may not realise how our conversations impact others. Our words can have unintended consequences.

Recently, someone let me know that something I'd said during a presentation had made them feel disempowered. Even though that had absolutely not been my intent, I had to own the fact that my words had created that feeling. And I deeply regretted it.

I was lucky that they drew it to my attention; usually, in situations like this, we are not told and can go through life unwittingly affecting how people think and feel (both positively and negatively).

Conversations are so important to building great relationships. If we can cultivate a deeper awareness of how our words are impacting others, we're more likely to be able to have engaged and trusting conversations and, in turn, stronger relationships. Often this is about being alert to body language, or what's not being said.

A challenge that all of us will come across at some point is how to give and receive feedback effectively. Just the word 'feedback' can trigger anxiety, so it's important to learn how to communicate in ways that are open, transparent and congruent.

Feedback in an environment that feels unfair or judgemental creates distrust and triggers our amygdala, that part of the brain that creates fight, flight or freeze responses when we feel threatened.

Conversely, an environment of openness and honesty triggers the receiver's pre-frontal cortex (the brain region for higher-level thought), allowing them to trust the feedback, even if they don't necessarily like what is being said.

Amygdala hijack

I remember many years ago taking my toddler twin boys and my mother to a major shopping centre (I know…what was I thinking!). While I ordered sandwiches and drinks in a crowded food court, my mother (I thought) was watching the boys in their pram. Before I could pay, my mother's hand shot out in front of me with the money. When I turned around to ask what she was doing, I saw the pram was empty!

The boys had disappeared while we were both distracted. During the busy lunchtime no staff were able to help us look for them and I started to panic. In fact, I was in a complete state of shutdown as cortisol coursed through my body. The only sensible thing to do seemed to be to lie on the floor and kick and scream to get some help (I didn't do this fortunately).

The good news is that they weren't kidnapped or out in the carpark; they had simply been attracted by a book shop and were down the back of the store looking at children's books. It was the most stressful five minutes of my life!

This is an example of amygdala hijack. In the work environment, people can experience something similar (perhaps milder) when their boss says, 'I want to give you some feedback…'.

Any threat response will create an amygdala hijack. When it happens, our body is flooded with cortisol, a stress hormone produced by our adrenal glands. Cortisol mobilises energy so we are ready to fight or flee. It's an essential hormone for our survival.

However, as it prepares us for fight or flight, cortisol shuts down our brain's executive thinking area, the pre-frontal cortex, so we can no longer think creatively and logically.

When we continue to produce high levels of cortisol over a long period, it can weaken our immune system, cause inflammation, impact our memory and weaken our ability to think creatively or coherently.

Cortisol vs oxytocin

While cortisol shuts down our creativity, another hormone – oxytocin – does virtually the opposite. Oxytocin is a nurturing hormone; it's usually associated with childbirth, as it helps mothers bond with their newborn babies. However, all of us, not just new mothers, produce oxytocin when we feel safe, socially confident and trusted. The oxytocin causes us to be less anxious, to experience rapport with others and to feel energised.

The way we behave and how we interact with others can shift our body chemistry, by stimulating the production of either cortisol (stressful) or oxytocin (energising). We usually know when we are experiencing either: we feel bad, or we feel good.

When we engage harmoniously with others – whether it's with people we have just met, or with people we have known for a long time – we all produce oxytocin.

Research in neuroscience suggests that oxytocin may play a dominant role in the brain and the heart, regulating our need for social contact. Therefore, we need to focus on oxytocin-producing behaviours to create conversations that inspire transparency, relationship building, understanding, a shared vision of success, truth and empathy.

Oxytocin helps us to build social connections. We can change how we engage with others so that our conversations are more likely to produce oxytocin conversations. We can do this by:

- focusing on what the other person is saying: really listening to what is being said; listening with an intent to understand
- seeking to understand or hear what's not being said
- asking more open questions to extend their (and our) thinking
- remaining focused on what they are saying, rather than waiting for an opportunity to respond
- not concentrating on what we are going to say next
- being less critical and becoming more curious
- focusing on the conversation fully, rather than multitasking.

Curiosity enhances our ability to have oxytocin-rich conversations.

Curiosity

A client, Julie, was struggling in transitioning from working in an IT environment to a business environment. In her old environment she was a subject matter expert and had the answers. She found it very easy to communicate with, and be understood by, her people leader, who had a similar background. Having previously worked as a consultant, Julie was very used to having all the answers. However, in the business environment she found that she didn't understand the business leaders she had to deal with and they didn't understand the information she provided.

One of the first things I suggested to Julie was to become more curious and to ask her business leaders open-ended questions even if she felt she already had the answers. At first Julie was puzzled and couldn't understand why this would be useful, as she felt that she should have the answers.

Focusing on being curious and asking questions moves us into a curiosity mindset; we switch our focus from 'self' to become more attuned to the other person. This puts people into a more trusting and receptive state and builds understanding of what we each mean, allowing us to discover new ideas and thinking.

Julie came back and said, 'Is it really that easy?'. She had discovered that other people's ideas and thoughts enriched her own thinking and also led to deeper and more meaningful relationships.

Curiosity is a state of active interest and genuinely wanting to know more about something. It's about being open to uncertainty or unfamiliar experiences. It helps us raise our awareness of ourselves and others, and allows us to form more satisfying relationships as we demonstrate an openness and a genuine interest in others. When we are curious about others we ask more questions because we want to learn more about them.

Our powers of observation expand when we are curious, and we see things differently. Studies have shown that high levels of curiosity are connected to greater analytic ability, problem solving and overall intelligence. So, focusing on strengthening our curiosity makes us smarter!

Being curious allows us to discover new things or new ways of doing something; in contrast, being certain means that we feel we are right and doesn't allow opportunities to explore different ideas. When we stay in our comfort zone we are unable to embrace curiosity.

According to the VIA Strengths Inventory the two main components for curiosity are: 1. people are interested in exploring new ideas and experiences and 2. having a strong desire to keep increasing knowledge.

Being curious and asking open questions to explore another person's thinking are some of the key ingredients for building trusting relationships. The importance of asking questions is summarised nicely in this quote, published in Michael J Marquardt's *Leading with Questions*:

> *A lot of bad leadership comes from an inability or unwillingness to ask questions. I have watched talented people—people with much higher IQs than mine—who have failed as leaders. They can talk brilliantly, with a great breadth of knowledge, but they're not very good at asking questions. So while they know a lot at a high level, they don't know what's going on way down in the system. Sometimes they are afraid of asking questions, but what they don't realize is that the dumbest questions can be very powerful. They can unlock a conversation.*

Trust is important to nurture curiosity. We want to be able to be curious and discover what others are thinking; we want to be able to expand our thinking. However, we need to feel safe so we can be vulnerable with each other, ask questions and be able to have robust discussions without fear about the impact on our relationships or our reputation. In a team we need to be confident that everyone's intentions are good, and we have no reason to be protective or careful around the group.

The more we are curious and help others to be curious, the stronger our relationships become – and that can lead to transformation

How to unleash our curiosity

Develop the art of asking powerful, sometimes provocative, and compelling questions. Questions are invitations into the world of curiosity; exploration through open-ended questions can lead to deep understanding.

This includes questioning 'normal' and people who say, 'this is how we've always done it' or 'we've tried this before and it didn't work'. Great questions to achieve this:

- Why can't we change how it's done?
- What if our assumptions were not true?
- What if the opposite were true?
- What other alternatives would work?
- How might we do this?

Consider whether you are asking because you already know the answer, or you are really curious about what the other person's answer could be?

Thrive on uncertainty. While uncertainty can make us feel uncomfortable, sitting in that feeling until it starts to ease can lead to lasting positive experiences.

Refer to the *Coaching Session* at this end of this chapter for ideas on how to expand your curiosity.

Focus on building rapport before asking questions. Rapport (which is covered in the following section) is about reducing difference between yourself and others and helps to make people feel safe.

Be open to sharing what you are thinking so that people start to understand why you have so many questions

Be careful, however, that your curiosity doesn't feel like an interrogation. Several Christmases ago at our family lunch, my niece had brought along her boyfriend who we hadn't met. He spent most of the meal not participating in our conversation. I started asking him questions about what he did, where did he lived, and so on. That is, until my brother told me to stop interrogating him!

Building rapport with the people we interact with and creating a feeling of safety is one way to prevent them feeling interrogated.

Rapport

Rapport can be defined as the ability to reduce difference between oneself and another at unconscious levels to promote a harmonious relationship.

Though it's often taken for granted, rapport is a foundation for good relationships. Even with people we don't like! Building rapport quickly with someone makes them feel that we are just like them.

When we have rapport with someone we feel safe to be curious; we listen more deeply, and trust builds between us. Being able to build rapport consciously is a technique we can learn – it will help us to forge trusting relationships, communicate effectively and work collaboratively.

A primary school vice principal hired me to help her change the first impression she was making during interviews. At the time we met, Linda had applied for nine principal roles for various schools in the Melbourne area. In each case she had come second. Applying and interviewing for a school principal role is lengthy, complex and difficult, so I really felt for her.

Linda wanted to focus on making a good first impression. The first thing I introduced her to was the concept of building rapport with someone, and how to do this within the first few seconds of her interview.

She was really curious about rapport and happy to try it out – choosing to practise with her new school principal, with whom she had a difficult relationship. As vice principal she had always been the sounding board for her previous principal, and this wasn't the case with the new principal, who was reluctant to share any information with her.

By practising rapport-building with her principal, and really entering her model of the world, Linda found that the principal was sharing information with her: they started trusting each other more, and their relationship improved substantially.

The great news is that, soon afterwards, Linda was successful at obtaining a principal role at another school.

We form impressions of people, events, and places within a few seconds

So, when you meet someone new, their impression will be determined by your first few words and actions.

It's mainly from the emotion generated in those first few seconds that people make meaning (good versus bad, 'like me' versus 'not like me') and our impressions are unlikely to change once we have made our instant assessment (remember the Ladder of Inference?).

Rapport is not about liking someone or agreeing with them (although it often happens naturally with people we like); it is not empathy or mimicking the other person. It is a technique to build a harmonious relationship with another person to facilitate effective communication.

We can actively and consciously build rapport with people, even when there's no previous connection or relationship. We can do this by:

- matching their physical gestures and posture
- matching the tone, pace, and volume of their voice
- matching their language
- matching the rhythm and pace of their breath

- matching their values or emotions.

This is something that occurs naturally. If we watch people on public transport who know each other, or people together in a restaurant, the rapport between them is unmistakable: when one leans forward, the other leans forward. When one crosses their legs, the other crosses their legs. There's a rhythm to the way they talk and do things.

By watching a person for non-verbal clues and listening for language patterns, we can adapt our own language and behaviour to harmonise with them and establish a deep level of rapport. This is accomplished through something called 'pacing and leading'.

In 'pacing', we pick up key verbal and non-verbal cues from another person and feed them back, to match their model of the world. Pacing, or matching, their non-verbal communication creates the sense that we are just like them. We essentially step into their shoes and communicate with them in their own way of speaking and through their own way of being.

'Leading' involves attempting to change, add to, or enrich another person's behaviour or thinking process by subtly shifting our own verbal and behavioural patterns in the desired direction, and having them follow.

We can use 'pace to lead' to test if we are in rapport. After pacing someone and matching them, we shift our posture. For example, if we are both leaning forward in our chairs, then I lean back, and they match my movement within a minute or so, and I move again, and they follow, and then again, as they continue to match our movement, I know that a level of rapport has been established.

When we consciously practise building rapport with others, it becomes automatic; then communication become easier and more effective, regardless of whom we are communicating with and our level of trust increases.

While my children were in primary school I was on the school council and became the president for a couple of years. Some of the parents and teachers on the council were very difficult to deal with. Many had joined the council primarily to meet their own agendas, which were often in direct conflict with the overall school council agenda. I used to feel physically ill every time the council met due to anxiety about what these councillors would do or say to disrupt our meetings.

Once I learned about rapport, particularly matching body language and pacing and leading, our council meetings ran more smoothly. I consciously built rapport with one parent in particular, then each other member of the council around the table, so in a short time everyone was in rapport. We could allow differences of opinion to co-exist with positive intent so that meetings no longer degenerated into discussions about personality.

Another client, Sam, was a country-based corporate manager who wanted to make some large changes to her life because what she was doing wasn't working anymore. She wanted to learn how to build rapport with everyone she came into contact with.

Up to a point Sam had been doing a reasonable job at managing her satellite business despite some challenging circumstances. Actually, her team was so dysfunctional that I'm surprised they managed to do all the great business they did! As soon as Sam learnt how to build rapport consciously, she found that all her relationships with family and the people she worked with changed, often in subtle ways. For want of a better word, they became 'easier'. She felt they understood her better, and she understood them better.

Think back to your work environment. Do you avoid communicating with certain people at work because you don't like them, or you just feel they are not on the same wavelength as you? Try building rapport with them. You may be surprised with the results.

Be aware of reducing differences to create a harmonious relationship and you can become known as that person who somehow gets along with everyone!

Refer to *the Coaching Session* at the end of this chapter for more ways to build rapport with others.

Your Personal Coaching Session

<u>Perceptual Positions Exercise</u>

Think about someone you regularly interact with. Practise mentally moving from first position, to third position (observer), to second position, back to third, and then to first position (back to you).

If you have a challenging meeting coming up, put yourself fully into first position by imagining that the people from that meeting are here right now and you are looking at them.

Now view the relationship as an observer from third position. Observe the interaction of the attendees of the meeting, including yourself, as if you were watching a video of the meeting.

Next, imagine that you are in another attendee's shoes (in second position). Look at yourself through their eyes. Assume the perspectives, beliefs, and assumptions of that attendee as if you were them for a moment. Repeat for the other attendees.

Review the information you have gained. What insights do you have about the experience? Has your own perception changed?

<u>Expanding your Curiosity</u>

Research a topic that interests you and drill down to get more understanding.

Provide the opportunity for people to share their curiosity with one another. Curiosity can be contagious; demonstrating our own curious mindset enables others to share their excitement and discoveries.

Do things differently from time to time. For example: use a different way to travel to work, or work from a different location.

Identify what's important; gain a deeper understanding of a topic that you are interested in and discover how you can apply it to your life.

Consider the list of low-interest, but necessary, activities in your typical day. Choose one of these dreary activities and, as you do it, search for any three novel or unexpected things about it.

When you talk to someone, learn as much as you can about that person and their perspectives. Give them space to really flesh out their ideas and ask follow-up questions to take their thinking further. Consider every conversation is an opportunity to develop your curiosity mindset and discover things that are thought-provoking.

Explore your environment and discover things you have never noticed before, that you either have ignored or taken for granted.

Get genuinely interested a few times a week in at least one of the many events encountered on a daily basis. Go deep on something you don't know or haven't thought about before.

In your relationships with others start to analyse your behaviour to find out what is working for you and what isn't, then keep practising what is working and decreasing what isn't working.

Think about what you add to the team conversation: are you extending the thinking or just agreeing with whatever everyone else says? Learn to develop your questioning muscle by asking questions about what is being said.

How to practise building rapport

Body Rapport

- Match posture.
- Match breathing.
- Match gestures.
- Match eye blink rate.
- Match spinal tilt.

Voice Rapport

- Match tone/pitch.
- Match volume.
- Match speed.

Practise by building rapport with each and every person you meet, everyone you talk to on the phone, even those people that you communicate with via email or other written correspondence. Wherever you are, notice the people around you. Notice if groups of people are in rapport.

CHAPTER 5

Flexibility and agility

I've been part of high performing teams a handful of times during my corporate career. The most memorable was when I joined a very small project management office team of three people, which managed a $3 million portfolio of projects. When I was brought in, the budget had just been tripled to $9 million and we didn't have a pipeline of projects.

Over the next three months we built the team to 40 people, comprising contractors and permanent staff, and it became one of the most enjoyable and high-performing teams I have been part of.

Our leader was open, transparent and inclusive, and willing to share any messages coming from the senior leadership group. We all had high levels of autonomy; the outcomes were directed but we had flexibility in how we achieved them.

We were adaptable, able to pick up work as required, and didn't rely on job descriptions to define what we did.

Almost everyone in our team had an open mindset. We were curious to explore how and what, and open to new ideas and new ways of doing things.

How we communicated and collaborated as a team was an area of active focus as the team grew. We were confident in each other's capability to do our job well and high levels of trust existed between us. The team pulled together during times of high stress and high workloads and also celebrated successes along the way.

When a team has this level of connection they can achieve far more than what is expected. Being flexible, both behaviourally and conversationally, we become more dynamic: we are able to respond in different ways, depending on what's needed (rather than falling back on how we've always done it). This characteristic of a high-performing team makes it a joy to be part of.

Behavioural flexibility

Many years ago, I had a particularly challenging relationship with a member of a committee I chaired. I perceived that Bob didn't value the opinions of anyone else on our committee and went out of his way to be difficult and challenging. My opinion was shared by most of the committee. As a result, our meetings became progressively more difficult and we achieved very little.

I had been learning about behavioural flexibility – being able to adapt our behaviour to suit the situation – so I decided to try it out with Bob. I focused on building rapport with him and changed how I responded to him during meetings: previously, I had angled my body away from him, totally minimised eye contact, and had enforced strict guidelines about how long anyone could talk about a particular issue to limit what he could say.

I consciously increased eye contact, faced Bob directly and listened deeply, then responded to indicate that I wanted to understand what he was saying. I also asked open questions (rather than trying to rush the conversation and move onto the next agenda item) to get him to really consider what he was saying.

Over the next few weeks and months, Bob's behaviour began to change, which created a bit of a snowball effect with other committee members as their behaviours also began to change.

We ended up achieving a lot of great things through that committee. And while I personally still don't like Bob, we found that we could work together constructively.

Behavioural flexibility is about varying our own behaviour to elicit a different response from another person. The change in our committee from low-achieving to high-achieving began, not with Bob, but with me changing the way I – as chair – behaved towards him.

When we are behaviourally flexible, we are able to react to a given situation in different ways, rather than falling back on habitual – potentially limiting – ways of reacting.

Repeating the same thing over and over and expecting a different result is the definition of insanity

If we get the same unhelpful behaviour from people when we interact with them, it's time to try something different to achieve a different result.

Imagine you have a tense relationship with a teammate: you believe that they don't respect you or value your opinion. How do you usually interact with them?

Are you defensive, or accusatory? Or do you avoid sharing your opinion (the silent treatment)? How could you act differently in your interactions to break out from these habitual, and maybe limiting, responses?

Think back to earlier sections where I described deep listening, perceptual positions, self-edit, the ladder of inference and building rapport. Each of these practices helps us adapt how our own behaviour to a given situation so that we are able to elicit more useful and resourceful responses from others.

Conversational agility

If you have ever practised yoga, you probably know that flexibility is key to mastering many yoga poses. Some people are naturally flexible; however, many of us only achieve flexibility only through regular practice. We all have the ability to increase our level of flexibility.

Likewise, our ability to think on our feet when talking with others – to be conversationally flexible – improves with regular practice. 'Conversational agility' is a phase used by organisational anthropologist and author Judith E. Glaser to describe our ability to reframe, redirect and refocus our own or other people's thinking to and move it into a different direction.

Another term for this is 'pattern interrupting': the idea is to assist the person we are conversing with to take a different perspective on what they think or believe.

Conversational agility is literally altering the description or context of a situation, usually to make it more acceptable. It can be used to place a concept, a behaviour, or an object in a more favourable light, or to draw attention to particular aspects.

When we are in conflict, creating a pattern-interrupt through reframing, refocusing or redirecting is a powerful way to have new insights. For example: if someone says 'I don't feel good about myself as I'm making so many mistakes', we can reframe this by saying 'When you make mistakes you're taking risks and that is how we learn. Think about the people from the past who have created amazing results, in spite of failing often'.

We can chunk the conversation up (to a more strategic, bigger picture level), down (into more detail) or sideways (to a different, yet connected, area). For example, if someone is spending too much time reworking something, rather than saying 'I'm really annoyed and how much time you are spending on this', refocus by saying 'You have such a high attention to detail and you really care about this piece of work. I'd love for you to apply this attention to detail to a number of new projects rather than just this one as you have a lot of expertise now'. This elevates them out of the place where they are stuck and moves them towards the bigger picture.

We can turn a difficult situation into an opportunity for finding trust and common ground by redirecting. For example: When they say, 'we couldn't have done anything differently' (stuck in the past), we might redirect their thinking by saying, 'I worked with someone who had the same issue and here is what they did to change it.' This creates a new way of looking at things.

Reframing, refocusing and redirecting can provide an opportunity for the person with whom we are talking to take a mental break and think in a new way. It can help shift someone who is distrusting, resisting or sceptical into a curious or co-creative mindset.

You can see how being flexible, both behaviourally and conversationally, enables us to respond resourcefully to different, and difficult, situations; we interact skilfully with others so that our performance, and that of others, increases. Our own flexibility helps others to change how they are being.

Awareness and listening is critical here: we need to be highly aware of ourselves and others, so that we can, firstly, see what needs to be said or done to achieve a particular outcome; and, secondly, adapt our behaviour as the situation changes.

Being aware of others – really listening to what they mean, trying to see things from their perspective, understanding our assumptions and how we jump to conclusions, questioning to clarify meaning – helps us to stay in tune with them; we can fine-tune our own behaviour in response.

It's in this sort of environment that we're more likely to have oxytocin-producing conversations, which prime our brains for creative thinking, and build trust, both of which are key enablers of high performance.

Practising awareness, and practising being flexible in our behaviour and agile in our conversations will help us to have more oxytocin-producing conversations and, ultimately, build teams that perform at the next level.

Your Personal Coaching Session

<u>Conversational agility</u>

The following provides examples of conversational agility so that you are able change the focus of your thinking or what other people are saying into something more resourceful and helpful.

If you or someone is stuck in how you are thinking, your ability to reframe, refocus or redirect may help yourself, and them become unstuck.

Example 1

Their comment: "I make so many mistakes and which means I'm afraid to try new things."

Your response: "When you do try new things and make mistakes, I see you learn from those and change how you do things – which means you are learning."

Example 2

Instead of saying: "You are spending too much time on the one project and redoing components when you should be focussing on more important projects."

Say: "Your attention to detail is wonderful; it shows how important it is to you and I would love you applying this same attention to other projects rather than just this one."

Example 3

Their comment: "We couldn't have done anything differently." (when something has gone wrong).

Your response: "Last week I worked with someone who had something similar happen. This is what they did – which is a completely new way of looking at things."

PART 3

US

US

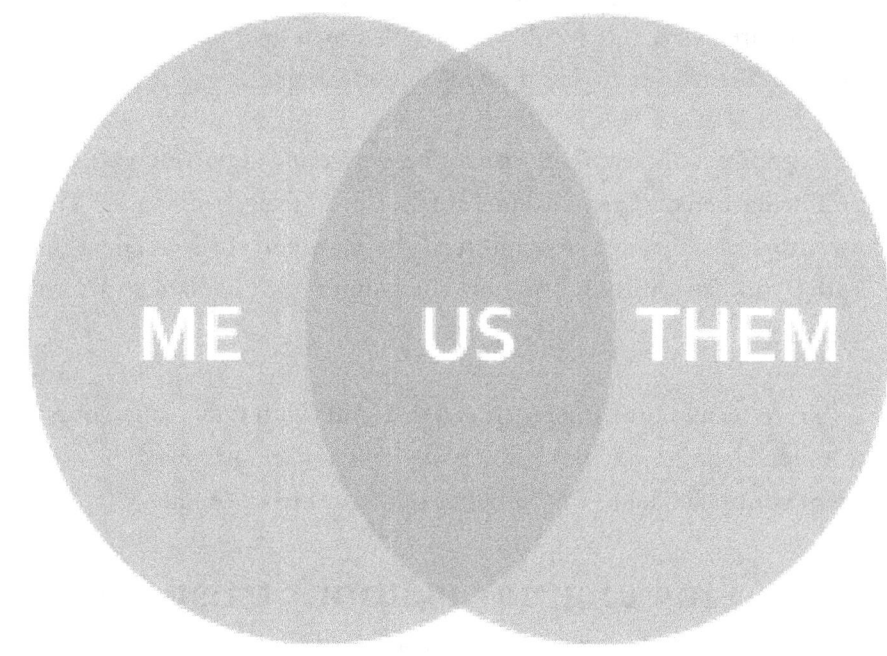

Figure 5: Me, Them, Us

Magic happens when 'me' overlaps with 'them' to create 'us' – high-performing, engaged and collaborative teams.

Being me-centric means I am too inwardly focused. Being them-centric means I am too outwardly focused. Being us-centric is the sweet spot that allows a team to be the best they can be individually and collectively, and to achieve amazing things.

Getting to 'us' is a journey. In the introduction, I described six different teams – toxic, frantic, erratic, authentic, energetic and dynamic – each at a different stage on the journey towards 'us'. The higher up this model a team is, the higher it's capacity to perform at a high level.

A team's performance often corresponds with the relative levels of cortisol and oxytocin among team members. Toxic teams can't perform because they are drenched in cortisol, which shuts down their pre-frontal cortex and prevents them from higher thinking and creativity.

So to improve our team's performance, we should aim to increase oxytocin-producing behaviours and limit cortisol-producing behaviours. There are ways to support our teams and turn them around. It is essential that as a leader you drive this and provide the support and guidance to your team members.

As we've seen in the earlier sections, this starts with tuning into yourself and to others, being conscious of they way you communicate and how you can adapt your behaviour to elicit better outcomes from others.

This chapter is about trust and engagement – building on what we've learnt to help take your team to the next level

CHAPTER 6

Trust

I once worked in a team where trust between two team members was broken. Even though it was not evident to others in the team, it meant that we never gelled as a team.

The term 'high-performance teams' is used a lot in corporations to describe teams that are highly focused on their goals, achieve superior results, and outperform similar teams.

There is no question that, among the high-performance teams I have worked with and observed, a high degree of trust exists between all team members. They watch each other's backs; their diverse skills and competencies complement each other; they openly share wide-ranging opinions; and they consistently communicate about any issues affecting the team.

Without trust, the team is simply a group of individuals doing their own thing. It doesn't matter how capable or talented each individual is; a team that lacks trust will not reach its full potential.

Neuroscience research indicates that trust and distrust activate different parts of the brain. Distrust is associated with the amygdala, the area of our brain triggered by stress, and leads to the cortisol production.

An atmosphere of distrust in a dysfunctional team is likely to mean that team members experience continued high cortisol levels; this would impact on their ability to think and reason effectively, since cortisol shuts down activity in the pre-frontal cortex, the brain's executive functioning area.

Using fear tactics to motivate others is often used in the workplace; however, this outdated way of leading is harmful – both to people, and to productivity – and has long-term consequences.

Research indicates that a main reason people resign is because of their manager's bad management skills, or bad behaviour.

In contrast, when we feel safe and trusted by the people we interact with, oxytocin is produced, which, in turn, increases social confidence and connection.

In this environment, team members support each other and are open and transparent. This leads to highly motivated team members who assume positive intent of others and focus on mutual success. They check for facts rather than making things up or listening to gossip. They keep promises and take a considered view to feedback.

Trust is required in any interaction we have with others if we are to reach an effective outcome. This is particularly true when we are part of a team. When we don't trust someone, the effect on the team can be dramatic.

I recently worked with a group of people brought together as a multidisciplinary team to pilot a new program. Midway through the 12-month pilot the team weren't travelling well. Communication was low, people did not trust each other's capability and collaboration between different areas was diminishing. The program was at risk of failing before the pilot was completed. While a number of factors contributed, distrust was central to the failure.

Fortunately, the team was committed to turning this around. They started by spending a day together to focus on how they were communicating (or not) and what was preventing them from collaborating effectively.

The outcome was that they set up more fluid ways of communicating that kept everyone continually updated about where they were at and what was next. They also reconfirmed their capabilities: everyone agreed that each team member was more than capable of doing their job well. This was the start of collaboration and trust building between team members. I'm excited about where they are going to end up.

Communication, collaboration and confidence in each other's capability are essential in a trusting environment; without them, it is difficult for a team to succeed

Communication

We can build trust through communication. Strategies and tools like deep listening, the ladder of inference and perceptual positions help us to become intentional about how we communicate, so we are likely to be more skilled at handling difficult situations with sensitivity.

Sharing information also helps to build and maintain trust. For example, if one team member discovers vital information that is relevant to the team's success, such as a deadline change or a lack of resources, they should communicate it to the other members as soon as possible.

Leaders often feel they need to protect their team from senior leadership directives and may prevent information passing on to team members. A term commonly used in the corporate environment is the 'cement layer' - a layer of middle management that stops messages being passed upwards and downwards. However, since openness and transparency are essential for trust, leaders must have confidence in their team's ability to handle communication from senior leadership.

A collaborative and trusting team environment allows team members to share personal information and develop a stronger bond with their teammates.

Collaboration

True collaboration won't happen without a sense of trust between team members. When team members collaborate, they share creative ideas without fear that another team member will take credit for their ideas. Team members who feel they are in a trusting team environment are more willing to bring up concerns that are relevant to the team's goals.

Collaborating team members are comfortable to have open debate with each other. Without it, there may be a lack of buy-in and commitment – for example, when there is token agreement on decisions but team members secretly (or not so secretly) plan not to follow through with what was agreed.

Capability

Team members must have confidence that their teammates are capable and can successfully complete the tasks relevant to the team's success. That way, each team member can focus on their own tasks without worrying about teammates following through with their assigned tasks.

However, when someone is struggling to do their role well, trust with other team members may be jeopardised, especially if they try to conceal it from the group. Team members must realise when they need help and ask for it. When team members show vulnerability to their teammates and the teammates respond in an efficient and helpful manner, trust will grow between them.

Building trust

Some people are very successful at building trust in their relationships. How do they do it? Does it just come naturally for some people and not others?

Effective leaders do not rely solely on talent that 'comes naturally'. If someone is good at something they have practised at a skill to become good at it. The musician is skilled at playing the guitar because they practise it every day.

Great leaders are skilled at building trust because they have practised it. They analyse their behaviour to find out what is working for them and what isn't; then practise the skills that work until they are so accustomed to them that, when it really matters, they instinctively perform them. In other words, they learn what works and then practise until it feels familiar.

Trust comes back to the way we relate to others: people who are successful at building trust practice being *reliable*, *accepting* of others, and *open*. As these behaviours tend to stimulate oxytocin production in the people with whom they interact, they help to build trust.

Reliability

People want to know if we do what we say we will do. It is pretty hard to have confidence in a person who makes promises they don't keep.

A close friend of mine told me about her mother who always used to promise to do fun things on the weekend with her when she was a child. Time after time, something would come up that meant it didn't happen. After a while, my friend didn't listen when the promises were made, as she knew it was unlikely to happen.

Reliability means following up and seeing through the promises and commitments made. It means 'I'll do what I say I'll do'.

If we work with someone that has a problem with reliability, we have to say something, or the relationship will suffer! A colleague I worked with was always late for our meetings, which made me feel that she didn't value my time. I started to become resentful and was reluctant to set up meetings with her. I finally explained that I felt she wasn't reliable. She was horrified and rectified the situation from that moment on.

This is a clear example of how someone being unreliable can upset the trust and collaborative nature within a team (and so compromise performance).

It's worth noting the way I communicated here too: I explained that *I felt* she wasn't reliable. I was very aware of how my words could impact our relationship. So I didn't say 'You're so unreliable!' in an exasperated voice, which would have caused a stress reaction. I provided feedback in an atmosphere of openness and honesty; and, although she didn't like what she heard, she accepted it and changed her behaviour. And the relationship remains strong.

Acceptance

Everyone wants to be accepted for who they are, not judged, criticised, or made to feel inferior.

Earlier, we discussed the power of words and how easy it is to inadvertently hurt someone by being careless with words. Using technical jargon or obscure references may cause someone to feel inferior or excluded if they are not familiar with them. Likewise, if we are not careful, we could give someone the impression that they are slightly stupid or inadequate because they don't understand some aspect of the company, department, or project as well as we do.

Avoid jargon, obscure references and in-jokes unless you are confident that everyone in the conversation is familiar with them. Practise deep listening: check in often to make sure people are with you (listening also for what's not being said).

Learn to value people with different opinions and perspectives. This is what a diverse workplace is all about: enriching our environment with different thinking. Using perceptual positions and stepping into other people shoes helps us to accept each other.

Openness

One of the best leaders I have worked with creates high trust with her teams. She has many team-building skills, including being very open. When there are changes, she shares pretty much everything that may happen, and her teams know that there will be no surprises.

People tend to want to cooperate best with people who will level with them and give them the whole story (even if some of the details may be unpleasant).

People can take good news or bad news, but they can't take surprises. If, as a leader, we discover a change of plans that will affect another person, or we are unhappy with someone's work, then we should tell them first. They will respect and trust us more for our openness.

Openness also means being straightforward and honest, and saying what is true even if it is unpleasant and not what the other person wants to hear.

When we practice reliability, acceptance and openness within our relationships we find that we become the kind of person people want to relate to. Each is important in order to build lasting, ongoing relationships – not one can be missing.

Think about your current team and other teams you have been part of, and what has contributed to trust-building within each team. How has reliability, acceptance, and openness applied to your individual relationships? How did they contribute to the team's performance? Was anything missing? Did that compromise the team's performance? How?

Think about how you can incorporate the following into your leadership style to build trust:

- Sharing information.
- Doing what you say you will do.
- Keeping promises, or explaining (being open about) why they can't be kept.
- Asking open questions to extend your and your team's thinking.
- Making everyone in the team feel valued.
- Noticing the reaction of the people you are interacting with: are they opening up or shutting down, when you speak?
- Eliminating words that create fear and distrust.
- Fostering inclusion of all team members.
- Appreciating and acknowledging team and individual efforts.
- Celebrating success.
- Encouraging team members to build on each other's capacity and capability.

When we focus on oxytocin-producing behaviours like those listed above, we are consciously building trust. Not only does our ability to connect lead to improved performance, but work is enjoyable as we hang out with a group of people we like. We feel trusted; we feel safe to explore, take risks, aim higher.

Refer to *the Coaching Session* at the end of this chapter to rate yourself on how reliable, accepting, and open you feel you are.

Your Personal Coaching Session

Consider how reliable, accepting, and open you feel you are. Give yourself a rating out of 10 for each (with 10 being expert) at home, and at work.

Reliability: 'I'll do what I say I will do'

- I take action
- I keep promises
- I meet deadlines
- I am punctual
- I follow up and follow through
- I deliver

Acceptance: 'who you are is OK with me'

- I respect other points of view
- I am empathetic
- I don't judge others
- I listen
- I allow mistakes
- I accept limitations
- I try not to change people
- I don't criticise
- I value opinions of others

Openness: 'I share my own thoughts and feelings'

- I clarify expectations
- I am willing to hear what others say

- My body language matches my behaviour/talk
- I am honest about my limitations
- I give and ask for feedback freely
- I'm a straight talker
- I don't play games or have hidden agendas
- I make rules clear

Is there a difference in how you scored yourself at home compared to at work? If so, think about how you could raise your scores where they are lower. Consider a time when someone lost your trust. What happened? What could you have done differently?

CHAPTER 7

Connect

In my work with organisations within Australia I'm sometimes asked to work with teams who have low scores from annual staff engagement surveys, and are required to identify actions to improve their engagement.

Many unhappy people come to work each day and do the best they can with their current mindset. But, as neuroscience research shows, it is very difficult to give our best with a disengaged and distrustful mindset.

Performance is linked to the quality of our connection with others. As we've seen, in a cortisol-rich environment, we live under a cloud of anxiety and don't look forward to work. Cortisol – which we produce during times of stress – lowers the collective intelligence of a team, as it stifles our ability to think strategically, logically and creatively.

How do we flip that around to create an environment that is rich with oxytocin, that nurtures teams and allows them to be dynamic, to be characterised by activity, change, progress, with positive, can-do attitudes, full of energy and new ideas?

We need to do more of the things that generate oxytocin and avoid things that cause the production of cortisol.

In the manic to magic model that I outlined in the introduction, the dynamic team is highly engaged. Team members trust each other. This is an oxytocin-rich and high-performing environment.

Two elements that help to connect this team and enable it to achieve are autonomy and clarity of purpose, which are explored below. However, perhaps at the heart of this team's success is the way they speak to each other. Later in this chapter, I will discuss how we can develop our conversational ability which I believe underpins the quality of our connections and, ultimately, our capacity for success.

Autonomy

My first job was as a receptionist in a forestry commission – a small office in a rural town. My role was a bit of everything – from typing letters, to leasing bee sites and tracking tree felling. Even though this was my first ever office role out of school, my boss gave me significant autonomy. He directed me as to what I needed to do, but left it up to me how I achieved that.

During the 12 months there I felt empowered and created several new and more efficient systems. I loved that role mainly due to the degree of trust and autonomy that was given to me.

In contrast, many years later, I worked for a small boutique coaching organisation, where the CEO was a micromanager. We always had to account for what we were doing and everything we did was reviewed and assessed. We were a small team and the stress levels were high amongst all of us. I ended up leaving before my 12-month contract finished as team morale was very low, we were always second-guessing, and the working environment was particularly stressful.

Lack of autonomy is known to reduce connection and engagement. Autonomy provides a sense of control over our role, which can affect our response to stress factors in our lives. When we feel more autonomous we are more resistant to stress; with less autonomy, we can perceive the same circumstances as more stressful. Micromanagement, therefore, can lead to low team morale, high employee turnover and less productivity.

While true autonomy can sometimes be hard to achieve in the workplace, a feeling of choice can be created. If you are a leader, give your team members room to do their job; treat them as individuals and coach them to reach their potential.

Put boundaries in place and, within those boundaries, allow individual team members to determine how they do their role. Being able to decide how you will complete a task or achieve a goal is intrinsically motivating.

This is exactly what my boss did when I started in a role created to manage a large complex portfolio of mining loans. I was given complete autonomy in how I set up this area. I was advised of the expected outcomes but how I achieved those outcomes was up to me. It was challenging and I was often pushed into my learning zone; however, I knew that I had the trust and backing of my manager.

On reflection, I realise that I loved both this and my forestry commission role because of the level of trust and autonomy I was given. I felt safe to experiment, and valued for what I achieved.

This means that investing in your team makes them feel valued and increases levels of oxytocin.

A sense of purpose also build connection with others.

Autonomy provides a sense of control over our role. As a leader, when you allow more autonomy in how the team achieves their outcomes you are creating an environment of safety and trust.

Refer to *the Coaching Session* at the end of this chapter for ideas on how to create more autonomy.

Purpose

"As a team what is our purpose and what are we here to do?

What is our focus?

What does success look like?"

These were the sorts of questions my colleagues and I were asking my manager and each other when I started a new role in a bank many ago. We were never able to reach a satisfactory conclusion, and other areas of the organisation were also confused about our purpose.

Without a clearly defined purpose and identity it is very difficult to feel engaged and have any sense of achievement. In his book *Start With Why* Simon Sine argues that people are inspired by 'the why': why our team exists, why we do what we do.

Knowing 'why' allows us to achieve remarkable things

In my new role we tried to define our purpose – our why – for 12 months. Without a focus and purpose we were directionless and certainly not inspired to do the best we could, because we didn't know what that was.

Understanding the 'why' of a team, or a goal or a task is important. However, don't assume the 'why' is obvious even if it seems so to you as team leader. Clearly communicate your purpose and defined outcomes and then leave it up to your team to work out how to achieve them. That demonstrates trust (that the team is capable of achieving the outcomes); it supports autonomy (set the direction then get out of the way); and it increases connection with the whole team.

Quality Conversations

When I read *Conversational Intelligence: How Great Leaders Build Trust and Get Extraordinary Results*, by Judith E. Glaser in 2015, it changed my business and influenced my future direction.

Judith is an organisational anthropologist who created the concept she calls Conversational Intelligence® (or C-IQ). I was privileged to train with her over two years and was in the inaugural group to be certified in Conversational Intelligence in 2016. The concept is summarised in Judith's quote:

To get to the next level of greatness depends on the quality of our culture, which depends on the quality of our relationships, which depends on the quality of our conversations. Everything happens through conversations!

Quality conversations is about connecting. It involves listening, clarifying and genuinely seeking to understand others

In doing so, it helps us to develop a shared reality, or a shared understanding. Working at the conversational level means that a change of culture is accessible to anyone.

We naturally converse on different levels. These are represented visually in the Conversational Dashboard™ shown in Figure 6.

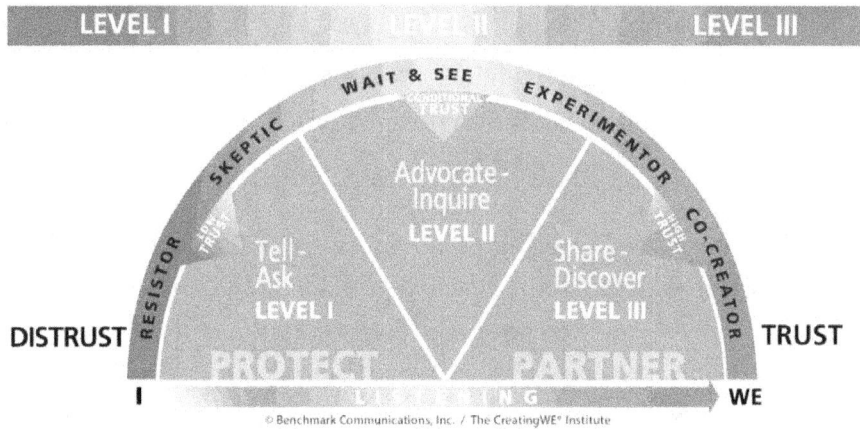

Figure 6: Conversational Dashboard

- Level I – Transactional. This level of conversation is I-centric. I have information to share with you and I will wait for you to pause in speaking so I can tell you. I am more focused on what I need to say than on listening to what you are saying. The need for trust is low; we are focused on validating and confirming our view of reality.

I used to spend a lot of time at Level I with my family, with conversations like: 'What will we have for dinner tonight', 'It's going to rain; make sure you take the washing off the line'!

At work, meetings can be transactional – checking action lists, updating each other and passing on information. There is a place for this level of conversation when we need to pass information on.

It's not always appropriate though: at its worst it can become the 'tell, sell, yell' syndrome (tell them once, sell them on the reason you are right, then yell when you think they aren't listening). This can increase cortisol (shutting down higher thinking) and lead to distrust.

- Level II – Positional. This is the level where we influence and defend what we know. We want to influence others to adopt our position. Trust at Level II is conditional: it may be there or not, as we have a desire to influence others to our point of view.

Again, there is a place for this level of conversation. We need to be able to influence others at different times, whether that's with our children to keep them safe or other people to persuade them to our point of view.

At its worst, Level II is where we can become addicted to being right and where we tend to ask questions we know the answers to and just want the other person to agree with us. We are influencing through personal or positional power.

This often occurs with teams in the relationship with their leader: if team members feel that their leader does not have their back or dictates how things should be done, trust levels may be low, which raises the level of uncertainty and that can trigger fear and cortisol production.

- Level III – Transformational. This is where we share ideas with others and discover what we don't know. This is Conversational Intelligence at its best. This level is characterised by high levels of trust and high levels of oxytocin; people feel they can share their inner thoughts and feelings. They feel safe to experiment, innovate and co-create, and they achieve results far beyond what they could have imagined.

I remember walking away from a meeting with someone I had met for the first time who was thinking about moving to Australia from Europe and realising that we'd had a transformational conversation. We had both been curious to discover what the other thought; the conversation had kept moving in new directions and had completely expanded our thinking. It had been energising and enlightening and we'd both walked away with new ideas.

Dynamics of meetings and our working life can change when we focus on tapping into each other's wisdom and insights and develop a shared idea of what success is. It's where we can be vulnerable and share our concerns without fearing that doing so could work against us.

At its worst a Level III conversation can become paralysis by analysis: we can spend too much time asking questions and taking the conversation further when we need to cut it off to move onto other things.

Whereas Level I conversations are all about me, Level III conversations are about us; they're saying 'let's work together' rather than 'I need to do this alone'. So let's see how Level I, Level II and Level III conversations might look in a weekly team meeting.

Consider the following scenarios:

- Each week we come together (usually reluctantly) and sit and listen to each person take turns to share what they've done for the week. This is simply an information download: no-one asks questions, people are checking their phones. The leader has several things to tell us, which don't require our input. Then it is our turn to give our updates. We all listen for the gap when the person speaking pauses, so we can jump in and say what we need to say. My attention is turned inward as I think about what I want to say when it is my turn; I'm not really listening to what others are saying.

This is a team meeting dominated by Level I conversations.

- Each week we come together for our team meeting. The meeting is dominated by the leader (or another team member) who has several agenda items to discuss. Technically, a number of decisions need to be made; however, as is the case in most of our meetings, the leader has already decided what they think is best and spends most of the meeting convincing us to agree with them. At times the discussion becomes quite heated until eventually we give in and go with what they have already decided.

This is a team meeting dominated by Level II conversations

- Each week we come together for our team meeting. The agenda is created prior with everyone contributing to what will be discussed or shared. We love these meetings as we each individually learn from the other team members and happily contribute our own ideas. There are always lots of questions which extends our thinking further. There is a real energy in the room. Everyone is comfortable to challenge other people's thinking and have robust conversations. We feel safe to speak up, happy to be vulnerable if we don't know something and we trust that others have our best interests in mind.

This is a team meeting dominated by Level III conversations.

Moving from the left side of the dashboard to the right side is key to improving team culture and performance. Level III conversations increase our oxytocin levels, which leads to more trust between team members, and enables us to engage our pre-frontal cortex – the part of our brain responsible for creative and logical thought.

In contrast, conversations that raise cortisol (which typically happen at Levels I and II), shut down our pre-frontal cortex, which decreases our ability to connect, be empathetic and work collaboratively.

A benefit of this model is that it helps people become aware of how they are communicating and provides a common language through which to identify and discuss their conversations. In doing so it establishes a pathway for change.

Awareness that conversations can trigger fear, power plays, uncertainty and the need to be right helps us to focus on what we need to change to have relationship building conversations, and consciously work towards transparency, understanding, empathy and a shared vision.

I recently worked with a very conservative not-for-profit organisation underdoing significant changes. Their new(ish) CEO was driving a new strategy that required many changes to the organisation. At a planning day, I drew the dashboard and asked the leadership group where they felt they were.

The CEO spoke up first and felt as a group they were in 'Experimentor' area (straddling Levels II and III). He was very excited about the changes, though a little frustrated in the laggard behaviour of his leadership group.

The rest of the leadership team suggested they were more in the 'Sceptic / Wait and See' area of the dashboard!

And just like that, the group saw visually what was going on. The CEO realised that he was well ahead in his thinking and needed to find different ways to engage his team. The team realised that they had been struggling as the CEO was well ahead of them in accepting these changes.

But having quality conversations isn't about just clicking our fingers and suddenly we can start to have Level III conversations.

For this team it meant that the CEO became more focussed on engaging directly with his team. He introduced regular team meetings and monthly one-on-ones. He put in a structure to create consistency with the message he was delivering about his vision for the organisation; as well, he provided regular feedback on what each person was doing well and acknowledging recent achievements.

Regularly asking 'where could we improve?', he provided constructive suggestions and encouraged team members to suggest improvements themselves. He also kept checking in to see how others were feeling about the changes as they progressed.

Back-and-forth discussions during team meetings became more generative: people were more comfortable to speak up and challenge others' thinking, and they became more curious, so asked more questions.

The energy in this team is changing as the team has more quality conversations more of the time, which have enabled them to move into a space where new ideas blossom and develop. The biggest impact has been the CEO slowing down and taking time to meet with his team and helping them throughout the change journey.

The team is feeling safe, trusted and willing to be a bit more vulnerable about how they are feeling about the changes. They now believe that the CEO has their back.

This example illustrates the way a leader can modify their own behaviour (to be more oxytocin-producing) in order to build trust and certainty in the team; and how this, in turn, transforms how the team engages and team performance lifts.

Conversely if the leader is more interested in being right or makes a comment that triggers fear (even if it is done inadvertently) then team members become less engaged, feel more at risk and levels of cortisol increases.

Putting it all into practice

You may be thinking about the reality of actually changing your conversations. Perhaps, in reading this book, you realise that you may have been unintentionally triggering fear or anxiety in your team. You may, for example, have a tendency to make critical comments: perhaps you set yourself high standards and have high expectations of others too.

It sounds easy to say, 'avoid cortisol-producing behaviour and focus on oxytocin-producing behaviour and relationship building', but how do you do that in the heat of the moment?

Changing your behaviour – becoming more flexible in your behaviour and more agile in your conversations –requires both self-discipline and self-control. (There is a subtle difference between these two.)

Self-discipline is about repeating positive actions consistently to achieve desirable behaviour. Self-control is about limiting or reducing undesirable behaviour. Both increase oxytocin and reduce cortisol.

Positive actions might include remembering to thank someone for helping us, checking in with colleagues to see how they're going, and encouraging everyone's participation when we chair meetings. Having the self-discipline to repeat such actions consistently builds trust and leads to more Level III conversations.

We display self-control when we stop ourselves from doing what we may previously have done automatically, like being overly critical of someone's work, raising our voice when people don't agree with us, or not listening and talking over people during meetings. These undesirable behaviours lead to distrust; by replacing them with positive actions, we provide the conditions in which trust can develop and so lead to more Level III conversations.

The first step, though, is to become aware of how your behaviour is affecting others. This involves becoming aware of yourself: recognising that high standards are important to you, realising, perhaps, that you believe that people should respond to criticism by lifting their game and not take it personally.

And then start to take more notice of the people around you: listen deeply and check in to really understand what they are saying, notice how they respond, listen for what they're not saying.

Catch yourself before you make that critical comment that may offend them. This self-control will limit potential damage to your relationships with your team. Instead of criticising, build understanding by explaining why high standards are important to you.

These changes will move you towards more quality conversations; more Level III conversations.

When you invest in your team – with your time, by listening, by being curious and asking questions – you make them feel valued. Helping them to understand the 'why' and giving them the autonomy and freedom in how they achieve goals demonstrates trust and increases connection.

I recently worked with a team and watched them move from 'authentic' to 'energetic' on the manic to magic model. They are currently working to become 'dynamic'.

The team and the broader organisation were going through a major organisational restructure and their leader wanted to prepare them for what was coming.

They were already efficient and, while trust existed to some extent between most team members, there were a couple of people who didn't really trust each other. They were also working in silos – doing their own job without much awareness of how this connected with what other people in the team were doing.

Over a period of six months the team attended a series of workshops and coaching sessions focussed on building trust, changing how they communicated together and creating stronger relationships.

They started to really focus on the types of conversations they were having practice. Having a common language of how they wanted to communicate meant that they could ask for what they wanted; for example, they started going to meetings and saying 'let's have a Level III conversation around this and see where it takes us'.

Their awareness grew, both of themselves and others. This enabled them to articulate how they worked best and understand how others preferred to work; to know where their strengths lay and tap into others in the team with different strengths. Their listening changed: rather than just telling others what they needed to tell them, they started listening to what others had to say and checked that they understood first.

In time, they refreshed their team meetings to be more purposeful, and brought everything they were doing back to their purpose, which was now clearly identified.

Because of the trust that now existed, difficult conversations that used to be avoided in the hope the problem would go away (it never did) were now becoming robust conversations. They felt safe to speak up. These were productive Level III conversations in place of less useful Level I or Level II conversations.

The leader created more autonomy for team members by starting to delegate more work, setting clear outcomes with the team and leaving it up to them to decide how they completed their tasks.

The team is now more collaborative: sharing ideas and supporting each other. Trust has increased significantly between the team members. They have a much stronger sense of who they are, of their own strengths and values and those of their team members; they recognise how they can complement each other. I am starting to see the 'us' emerge from 'me' and 'them'.

This team is moving towards the dynamic level: they are starting to watch each other's backs, are more willing to share diverse opinions, and communicate consistently about issues that affect the team. They are also becoming curious about what else they can achieve.

Your Personal Coaching Session

Autonomy

You can nurture autonomy by:

- encouraging a learning mindset for yourself and your team
- listening to the team and what they have to contribute
- letting them share their expertise and ideas and try out new ways of doing things
- being OK for mistakes to happen and help the team learn from them.

CHAPTER 8

Us-centric

The first section of this book was about 'Me': finding a way to become what we need to be to get the best out of ourselves. It explored how to become more self-aware, and how to identify – and get to – our desired state from where we are now.

In 'Them', we looked at developing the skills to build relationships and interact effectively with others: the focus was on developing awareness of others.

The final section brings the two together: when it comes to leading a high performing team, the focus must be on 'us'. This is about putting our self-awareness and awareness of others into practice: being skilful about how we communicate – actively striving for Level III conversations to develop a shared understanding; building trust and promoting oxytocin release, which in turn facilitates creativity, collaboration and higher level thought.

We've seen that our relationships – how we interact with others – is key to moving our team higher on the manic-to-magic model. Working together in an environment of trust, creativity and shared purpose enables high performance; what's more, it's energising and a fun place to be!

As the leader, you can create the high-performing team you want to be part of. If your team is lower down the manic-to-magic model, it means there is room to move up. Focus on what you need to do, what your team members need to do and look at ways to get there.

- Be aware of your impact on others. Is your behaviour triggering oxytocin or cortisol in others (and in yourself)?
- Have more Level III conversations. Focus on listening to really understand what is being said. Be curious: ask questions to discover what other people are thinking. Check that you understand by clarifying meaning. Think about how you can reframe, refocus or redirect when appropriate.
- Build trust with your team and colleagues. Use the rapport building technique to reduce differences. Think about the data you are (unconsciously) selecting to build beliefs or support beliefs you may have about others.
- Make team meetings collaborative and action-oriented. Involve your team in redesigning how they are run.
- Empower your team by delegating and giving them more autonomy. Make sure they know you are there to support them.
- Be prepared to have difficult conversations. Don't allow bad behaviour to continue and diminish the trust of the team.

Let's move away from a toxic culture where people feel unsafe to address concerns or hold others accountable, and move towards a trusting culture that people enjoy and where success thrives.

It's worth it for you, your team and your organisation!

NEXT STEPS

If you're serious about lifting your leadership to the next level and creating the type of culture you want to be part of - then use the concepts introduced in this book. Pick one of two that immediately resonate with you and put them into practice.

If you need some help to build more understanding of you (the 'Me' section), or more understanding of the people in your team and your stakeholders (the 'them' section) and how to bring 'Me' and 'Them' together and create that amazing 'Us' - contact me as I would love to work with you.

My intention in writing this book is to make your life and work more fulfilling. Did it work?

Feel free to share this book with your team and your peers, you don't have to do this alone.

Let me know how you are going.

Thanks.

maree@mareeburgess.com
www.mareeburgess.com
FB: https://www.facebook.com/burgessmaree/
LI: https://www.linkedin.com/in/mareeburgess/
Insta: maree_burgess

SOURCES

INTRODUCTION

The average person will spend 90,000 hours at work over a lifetime – a third of our lives. Andrew Naber, Gettysburg College

CHAPTER 1

Daniel Goleman, Emotional Intelligence – Why it can matter more than IQ. 1996

"Story of the Engine That Thought It Could", New-York Tribune 1906

The Deloitte Millennial Survey 2018 shows millennials place a premium on finding an employer whose guiding principles reflect their own

Peterson, C., & Seligman, M. E. P. (2004). Character strengths and virtues: A handbook and classification. New York: Oxford University Press and Washington, DC: American Psychological Association.

VIA Strengths Inventory: http://www.viacharacter.org/www/Character-Strengths Survey.

Online Strengths Finder: https:// gallupstrengthscenter.com. Created in 1998 by Donald O. Clifton PhD with Rath and scientists from Gallup.

Daniel Goleman, 'Emotional Intelligence: What Makes a Leader?' *Harvard Business Review*, 1998.

The XX Project - http://mareeburgess.com/shop

Bandler & Grinder (1979) Frogs into Princes

CHAPTER 2

C Dweck, Mindset: How You Can Fulfil Your Potential - Robinson, 2012.

de Berker, A. O. et al. Computations of uncertainty mediate acute stress responses in humans. (2016). https://www.nature.com/articles/ncomms10996

CHAPTER 4

Oscar Trimboli, Deep Listening: Impact Beyond Words, 2017. https://www.oscartrimboli.com/deep-listening-book/

The 7 Habits of Highly Effective People, 1989, Stephen Covey.

Perceptual Positions - Neuro Linguistic Programming (NLP).

Ladder of Inference, Chris Argyris. The Fifth Discipline Fieldbook: Strategies and Tools for Building a Learning Organization (Peter Senge, Richard Ross, Bryan Smith, Charlotte Roberts, Art Kleiner).

Green, Mitchell, "Speech Acts", The Stanford Encyclopedia of Philosophy (Winter 2017 Edition), Edward N. Zalta (ed.), https://plato.stanford.edu/archives/win2017/entries/speech-acts/.

Curious? Discover the Missing Ingredient to a Fulfilling Life by Todd Kashdan, PhD (HarperCollins, 2009).

VIA Strengths Inventory: http://www.viacharacter.org/www/Character-Strengths Survey.

M J Marquardt Leading with Questions: How Leaders Find the Right Solutions By Knowing What to Ask, Jossey-Bass, 2014

Rapport definition taken from Neuro Linguistic Programming.

First impressions: Making up your mind after 100 milliseconds exposure to a face. Janine Willis and Alexander Todorov, Princeton University. July 2006 Psychological Science

CHAPTER 5

Judith E. Glaser, Conversational Intelligence: How Great Leaders Build Trust. Bibliomotion; (2014)

CHAPTER 6

What Does the Brain Tell Us About Trust and Distrust? Angelika Dimoka *MIS Quarterly* (2010)

Stress signalling pathways that impair prefrontal cortex structure and function. Amy F. T. Arnsten. Published: 01 June 2009 Nature Reviews Neuroscience volume 10

Gallup poll 2013 concluded that the No. 1 reason people quit their jobs is a bad boss or immediate supervisor.

The Trust Factor. Paul J. Zak PhD. Published 2017

Lead at Your Best Joanna Barsh and Johanne Lavoie. Article McKinsey Quarterly April 2014

CHAPTER 7

S Sinek, Start With Why: How Great Leaders Inspire Everyone to Take Action, The Penguin Group, 2009.

Conversation Dashboard™, Judith E. Glaser, Conversational Intelligence How Great Leaders Build Trust. Bibliomotion; (2014).

www.ingramcontent.com/pod-product-compliance
Lightning Source LLC
Chambersburg PA
CBHW072042290426
44110CB00014B/1552